"All it takes is one column to pull you in. Rich in humour, overflowing in ideas. This is Jaime Watt at his candid best."
—*The Right Honourable Brian Mulroney, PC, CC, GOQ, 18th prime minister of Canada*

"Astute analysis. Profound empathy. Uncompromising honesty. *What I Wish I Said* has it all. Jaime Watt has the unique gift of bringing together diverse perspectives and making sense of the chaos. His writing is essential reading for anyone who wants to understand the political landscape today."
—*Lisa LaFlamme, OC, OOnt, Canadian journalist*

"I'm told I only have 35 words to comment on Jaime's book: heartening and heartbreaking, thought-provoking, thoughtful, funny, on target, elucidating, progressive, compassionate, and purposeful. A retrospect that looks forward—and is well worth looking into."
—*Jordan Bitove, publisher of the* Toronto Star *and owner of the Torstar Corporation*

"Jaime Watt is a political insider who knows exactly what people on the outside are thinking. You can disagree with him, but you would be foolish to ignore him. His writing is always insightful and, of course, entertaining."
—*Rick Mercer, OC, comedian, television personality, political satirist, and author*

"It's easy enough to brag about what you get right, but it's hard to be honest about what you get wrong. Jaime Watt threads the needle on both with his *Confessions of a Columnist*. A fun, revealing, and smart read."
—*Peter Mansbridge, OC, award-winning journalist*

"More than most, a Jaime Watt column requires you to read between the lines. He's in the know on so much that never gets published, so I look for the hints and clues to what lies beneath."
—*Phillip Crawley, CM, CBE, publisher and CEO of the* Globe and Mail

"To write a regular column is to tap into a certain amount of fortitude. To revisit columns past, as Jaime Watt does here, is to really show a firmness of spirit. The result is a timely, purposeful retrospective."
—*Kyle Wyatt, editor-in-chief,* Literary Review of Canada

"Political commentary, delivered with depth, insight, and empathy. He has a unique ability to distill complex issues into accessible, thought-provoking ideas that challenge our assumptions and encourage us to see the world from different perspectives. A must-read for anyone interested in politics and public affairs."

—*The Honourable Mike Harris, OOnt, 22nd premier of Ontario*

"I have watched with interest as Jaime has grown from partisan political warrior to trusted adviser to senior Canadian statesman/commentator. This is Jaime at his deep, kind, and honest best!"

—*The Honourable David Peterson, PC, KC, OOnt, 20th premier of Ontario*

"Very infrequently in life do we get the chance to 'do over' something from our past. Jaime Watt has created this opportunity, and all of us benefit. I love that we can hear Jaime thinking about what he got right and what he didn't. Maybe he will set a precedent for other columnists. The whole world of political opinion would be the better for that!"

—*The Honourable Kathleen Wynne, 25th premier of Ontario*

"In our time of information overload, Jaime offers thoughtful consideration. His even-keeled perspective stands out from the stridency that too often characterizes today's commentary."

—*The Honourable Dalton McGuinty, OOnt, 24th premier of Ontario*

"I've worked with Jaime Watt across many different fields of endeavour and have always valued his opinion and advice. An illuminating and highly engaging book."

—*The Honourable Ernie Eves, OOnt, KC, 23rd premier of Ontario*

"Jaime Watt's book is a tour de force of political commentary. His keen observations and razor-sharp analysis offer a unique perspective on the world of politics and the media. This book is a must-read for anyone interested in the inner workings of the political machine."

—*The Honourable Alison Redford, ECA, KC, 14th premier of Alberta*

"Jaime Watt's writing is a masterclass in political commentary—thoughtful, nuanced, and always compelling. His ability to cut through to the heart of the matter is truly remarkable."

—*The Honourable Jean Charest, PC, 29th premier of Quebec*

"I have known and respected Jaime Watt for many years. Anything to which he adds his name, be sure to read it. Whether you agree or disagree with his arguments, the read is well worth the time spent. And his thoughts always stimulate one's thinking."
—*The Honourable Margaret McCain, CC, ONB, 27th lieutenant-governor of New Brunswick*

"Thoughtful, nuanced, and always compelling. *What I Wish I Said* is a unique take for columnists—interesting, surprising, and entertaining to the max."
—*Sally Armstrong, OC, Canadian journalist and human rights activist*

"Jaime Watt's columns served as a compass for me, an immigrant to this incredible yet complex country, in my pursuit of becoming a better Canadian. For anyone who is new to Canada and navigating its intricacies, this book and Jaime's columns are essential reads."
—*Bob Dhillon, OC, founder, president & CEO of Mainstreet Equity Corp.*

"*What I Wish I Said* is an open invitation to join the conversation that shapes our public life. Jaime Watt thinks beyond clichés and asks: 'What do you think?' It's well worth the time and the thoughts it provokes."
—*Gordon Campbell, OC, OBC, 35th mayor of Vancouver and the 34th premier of British Columbia*

"Jaime Watt and I are not always on the same political page, but I have learned to admire his humility and wisdom. He is also a man of great humanity and good humour."
—*The Honourable Bob Rae, PC, CC, OOnt, KC, Canadian ambassador to the United Nations, 21st premier of Ontario*

"Jaime Watt has earned his reputation as one of Canada's sharpest communicators. His skill is married with passionate beliefs, which pop off the page in this book. He and I have been both adversaries and allies, but I have always admired the depth of the convictions with which he argues in these columns."
—*The Honourable Jason Kenney, PC, ECA, 18th premier of Alberta*

"Jaime Watt's writing is a refreshing blend of wit and wisdom. His columns are always thought-provoking and insightful, and this book is no exception."
—*The Honourable John Baird, PC, former Canadian minister of foreign affairs*

What I Wish I Said

Confessions of a Columnist

———

Jaime Watt

with Breen Wilkinson

OPTIMUM
PUBLISHING
INTERNATIONAL
LONDON I MONTRÉAL I TORONTO

What I Wish I Said, Confessions of a Columnist
© Ottawa, 2023, Jaime Watt and Breen Wilkinson

FIRST EDITION

Published by Optimum Publishing International
Dean Baxendale, President & CEO
Toronto, Canada

LIBRARY AND ARCHIVES CANADA CATALOGUING IN PUBLICATION
Title: What I Wish I Said, Confessions of a Columnist
Jaime Watt with Breen Wilkinson
Names Jaime Watt, 1958 author. | Breen Wilkinson, 1994, author.

Subjects: Politics, Government, Leadership and Civil Liberties
What I Wish I Said, Confessions of a Columnist
Description: Optimum Publishing International Canada edition

ISBN 978-0-88890-346-4 (Paperback)
ISBN 978-0-88890-347-1 (Hardcover)
ISBN 978-0-88890-3488 (ePub)

Editor: Margo LaPierre
Designer: Vahagn Stepanian
Typesetter: Jessica Albert
Author photography: V. Tony Hauser

PRINTED AND BOUND IN CANADA

For information on rights or any submissions, please e-mail
deanb@opibooks.com
Optimum Publishing International

www.optimumpublishinginternational.com
www.whatiwishisaid.ca
Twitter @opibooks | Instagram @opibooks

For Paul,
the love of my life,
who gave me life.

Acknowledgements

As a first-time author, I found the journey of writing this book to be surprising. Some things quite easy. Others, much harder.

This page is harder.

How to put into words, how to adequately thank those who have not only given me so much but who have made this book, at its core, possible.

So, knowing that I will not do them the honour they have done me, let me start.

First, special thanks to André Pratte and Michael Cooke. Companions through this journey—among many others—they are the gentlemen who told me this was all possible in the first place. That there was a book in the idea and that it didn't have to just stay a dream.

If this book makes sense as you read it, if it is coherent, it is as a result of the astonishingly good work of Margo LaPierre—a poet in her own right. Her perspective of her role as an "e" editor rather than an "E" editor allowed her to make crucial improvements while still allowing it to be my book.

If you think the book is as beautiful as I do, it is due to the work of Vahagn Stepanian. I am deeply grateful for his attention to detail, creativity, and willingness to continually refine his design until it was perfect.

Beautiful books only come to life with the support of an experienced and thoughtful publisher. Dean Baxendale is both. I am indebted to him.

Now, just as no one thinks Michelangelo painted that whole ceiling himself, no one thinks I write the column all by myself. And that's because

I don't. This whole project—the weekly columns—has only been possible because I have had the help of many, many Navigator colleagues over the years. Among them: Thomas Ashcroft, Simon Bredin, Andrew Galloro, Ryan Guptill, Travis Kann, Michael Stock, and Connor Whitworth. I also want to express my thanks to the entire team at the *Toronto Star*—past and present—who've helped edit this column over the years, particularly Scott Colby and Joe Howell.

Additional thanks are due to Jeff Costen for his keen editorial eye as well as his willingness to read a penultimate version. To John Wilkinson for agreeing to do the same. To Jackson Bovey for helping with writing at crunch time. And to Kyle Jacobs who kept me on track, or rather, keeps me on track, so that I am able to get anything done.

And, of course, to my co-author Breen Wilkinson—yes, that is his dad who pre-read the book. Breen is, simply put, an astonishing, once-in-a-generation talent. No Breen, no book.

And finally, this book was only possible because the late John Honderich, CM, OOnt, long-time publisher of the *Toronto Star*, asked me in September 2016 to write a weekly column in what was then the *Star*'s Politics page.

Writing this column became, for me, a cherished perch, one that I embraced with genuine enthusiasm as I wrote every week.

That enthusiasm was always matched by John, who was not only a terrific cheerleader but a great friend. Like so very many, I miss him very much and hope that this book can be considered, in a modest way, a tribute to him.

Jaime Watt

Jaime Watt is the Executive Chairman of Navigator and Founder of the Canadian Centre for the Purpose of the Corporation. He specializes in complex public strategy issues, serving both domestic and international clients in the corporate, professional services, not-for-profit, and political leaders at all three levels of government across Canada. Jaime currently serves on several boards, including the University Health Network and the Shaw Festival. As chancellor of OCAD University and an adjunct faculty member of the Directors Education Program at the University of Toronto, Jaime is committed to developing Canada's next generation of leaders. A sought-after public affairs commentator and weekly columnist for the *Toronto Star*, Jaime regularly shares his expertise and insights with audiences across Canada.

Breen Wilkinson

Breen Wilkinson is a Consultant at Navigator with over six years of experience at Queen's Park in strategic communications and engagement. Breen holds a master's degree in English literature from McGill University and an Honours Bachelor of Arts in Philosophy and English literature from the University of Toronto.

Contents

Part 3: In Power

Part 4: In Opposition

Part 5: The Trump Years

Part 6: The COVID-19 Crisis

Foreword

The Art of Opinion Writing

André Pratte,
former columnist and chief editorial writer at
La Presse and former senator

I knew Jaime Watt's reputation before I came to work for him at Navigator, the firm he launched two decades ago. I quickly realized that what people said about Jaime—that he is a brilliant political strategist and crisis manager, a true conservative, and a committed progressist, an innovative businessperson, an unstoppable workaholic, a man of vast culture—was all true. Jaime is passionate about his business. He demands the same from his employees, but he is also fair and understanding. You can sense all those qualities when you read his weekly commentary in the *Toronto Star*.

If you haven't had the chance to read his texts in the *Star*, this book is a great opportunity to discover one of Canada's most thoughtful commentators. Even if you are an avid reader of his columns, you will find great pleasure in reading them again, for they are as fresh now as when they were written. Jaime Watt has mastered the art of opinion writing.

But how does one master this art? Some young journalists dream of becoming an investigative reporter. Others hope to travel the world, reporting on wars, famines, and mass migrations. A few aspire to become an opinion journalist. I was part of that last group.

In 1975, then an economics student at McGill University, I sent *Le Devoir* a short letter regarding the announcement that Queen Elizabeth would open the 1976 Olympics in Montreal (I was opposed). The letter was published a few days later; this was the first time I expressed an opinion to a large public. Encouraged, I sent a second letter. This one was never published. My disappointment gave way to astonishment when I received a letter signed by *Le Devoir*'s revered director, Claude Ryan, explaining why he had decided against publishing my epistle. I could not believe that Mr. Ryan had taken the time to write to an unknown eighteen-year-old! Mr. Ryan was my model then, and he still is, although he passed away many years ago.

It would take more than twenty years before I would have a second opinion piece published in a newspaper; by then, I had been promoted to a columnist position at *La Presse*.

Opinion writing can be an extreme sport. Mostly, however, it is an art. The "opinion" part is important, of course, but the "writing" is crucial. A well-written column will be much more effective at broadcasting the author's opinion than a poorly drafted one. Although this point appears obvious, it is not. The reason is that writing well is more difficult than most people realize. It is not only a matter of spelling and grammar, it's a matter of style.

I always thought that a well-written column or editorial is not one that convinces the reader to change his or her mind but one that helps them make up their own mind by providing reliable information and rigorous reasoning. Mr. Ryan's editorials always had the same structure, which I am unashamed to say I tried to imitate:

- Introduction: What's the issue?
- One possible way of seeing the matter
- The alternative way of looking at it
- Mr. Ryan's reasoning
- Conclusion: What's his opinion?

It always appeared that *Le Devoir*'s director had done more research and knew more about the issue than all other commentators combined. Many disagreed with Ryan. But all came to respect him.

———

I began my career in radio in the mid-1970s, working for what was then a major Québécois radio station, CKAC Montreal. Luck struck in 1980 when I was sent to Ottawa to cover Parliament Hill. The topics to be covered were complex, controversial, and fascinating: the Constitution, the National Energy Program, Trudeau's "peace tour," the Clark-Mulroney fight to the finish, John Turner's return to politics.

Though I was only in my early twenties, I began being invited onto television shows to comment on political events in the nation's capital. After Brian Mulroney was elected as head of the Progressive Conservatives, I opined that with such a weak leader, the Tories would never form the government. I was at once unbelievably pretentious and very, very wrong.

I began writing as a freelancer for the weekly *Dimanche Matin*, then for Quebec's foremost daily, *La Presse*. I discovered then a passion for writing, a format that allowed me to say so much more than radio stories did. Those were often too short to allow one to explain what was going on.

I was not a guy to get scoops or be a muckraker. It is policy that fascinated me, not politics.

I was hired by *La Presse* in 1986. My aim remained the same: one day, I hoped to be an editorial writer. After several ups and downs, my dream came true in 2001. Despite my shortcomings, I was unexpectedly appointed *La Presse*'s chief editorial writer, a position that I proudly held for fourteen years.

It is an extraordinary privilege to be provided with a prestigious platform from which one can express her or his opinion on a regular basis. It is also a heavy responsibility toward the readers and the organization you work for. Those who take this responsibility seriously swear an implicit oath to be truthful and rigorous.

In the long run, people will read your articles only if they trust you. If you are well-known for your experience and commitment, you will enjoy the trust of many readers right from the start. Such was the case with Jaime Watt, who had accomplished so much in his career when he began writing for the *Toronto Star* seven years ago. If, like me, you are an obscure reporter, you must earn that trust. The process is long and arduous. In either case, one ill-advised column can irremediably break the readers' confidence.

Over the years, my passion for writing continued to grow. I wrote editorials, I wrote speeches, I wrote books. I experimented with writing tweets, but those are too short, too spontaneous for my taste. Writing requires reflection; that demands time.

Speaking is not as demanding. Talking heads on television say all kinds of things that are as quickly forgotten as they are stated. Not so with writing: your reasoning must be foolproof, your facts, 100 percent accurate. Once it is published, your opinion is available to be analyzed, criticized, judged. One mistake, and the whole edifice collapses.

I once wrote an editorial about hockey where I mentioned that Mario Lemieux wore number 77. In fact, as my eldest son did not fail to remind me, 66 was the number embroidered on Lemieux's jersey. Most readers got the impression that I knew nothing about sports and that I should not have ventured on such slippery ground; the readers were right.

———

I mentioned the late Claude Ryan, long-time director of *Le Devoir*. Thanks to his formidable intellect, Ryan was one important reason why the Montreal daily was reputable. Not only were his clear-cut editorials widely read, but politicians consulted him on a regular basis. A government's life was made much easier if Ryan approved of its policies.

I never had that kind of impact during the fourteen years that I led *La Presse*'s editorial team. Nowadays, columnists, with their personal, emotional style, have a lot more influence than editorialists do. Moreover, television and radio news personalities are the ones that politicians consult and fear.

The Internet and social media have transformed the world of opinion. In the old days, if a reader was angry at what an editorialist had written, they had to fetch a piece of paper, write a letter, put it in an envelope, find a stamp, and mail it. Today, one can quickly send an email (opinion jour-nalists receive hundreds of those a day); even more effective, they can write a furious tweet.

When I was at *La Presse*, at least 40 percent of Quebecers were sep-aratists, including a strong majority of the province's intellectual class. I tried to convince our readers that Quebec was stronger within Canada than it would be as an independent country. I praised the Canadian adventure and extolled federalism's virtues.

Even if I did all this in the most respectful manner, to a large number of readers, I became the enemy. I received my load of angry emails, and with social media, the tone grew increasingly aggressive.

I left *La Presse* eight years ago and am still seen by many as a traitor to the nation and a puppet of the wealthy Desmarais family, then the paper's owners. My case is far from unique. Indeed, in today's polarized world, it is the lot of all commentators, including the more moderate, respectful ones. An insult-proof vest has become a required tool of the trade. Yet, I am convinced that even in today's world, the reasonable written word remains uniquely powerful, an irreplaceable guide for concerned citizens and democratic governments.

Preface

History on the Run

Many writers fear the blank page.

I understand.

Sort of.

For me, there's a greater, more oppressive terror: four p.m. on Friday. Because, just as it happens on those television cooking shows when the bell rings and the contestants' hands go up, that's when "send" is clicked and the column is filed—ready or not.

And it is then that my mind is flooded with all the things I wish I'd said.

It is, you see, a button of no return. Clicking "send" is a necessary, time-bound decision. While often terrifying, these are conditions in which I've thrived, made my living, won a few friends, and influenced people.

In this way, my day job as a strategist not only helped me get my start as a columnist but also prepared me for the challenges to come. That's because a strong column relies on a swiftly developed and definitive stance, a firm and explicit point of view. It depends on brevity and simplicity. There's no space for endless detail, complexity, or equivocation.

And all columns, be they strong or plain rotten, must be filed *on time*. There are no second chances. No opportunities for a last-minute revision. And that pretty much describes what I do every day—the pursuit of perfection against the clock.

Of course, I don't know everything about the art of column writing. I am still learning. But when the minute hand is ticking to the top of the hour, and four p.m. is looming, I do know this:

It's stand and deliver.

It's black or it's white.

It's a column, on deadline, in 650 words or less, or it's nothing at all.

Oh, and the next morning, I'll be consumed with what I wish I'd said.

———

Journalism is, as the cliché goes, history written on the run. In writing a column for the *Toronto Star* these past seven years, I have tried to do just this.

I attempted to offer insight on the most pressing events as they were still unfolding. I tried to ask the questions no one else would or could. And I sought to break the mould of consensus encrusted around the Canadian opinion sphere.

In so doing, I have been proven both mercifully right and magnificently wrong.

But this is the beauty of columns. Everything that makes them so extraordinarily challenging simultaneously makes them uniquely powerful and fulfilling. The time pressure can be electrifying. The high expectations of your readers can push you to perform. And the privilege to write about real and vital events shifting beneath your feet, and to be among *the very first* to do so, can be—and often is—deeply humbling.

So, despite all the risks and challenges involved, I have come to know column writing as a rich and rewarding art but, more importantly, one that matters to our civic life.

As columnists, we are often thrust onstage with only half the story but must deliver our perspective, nonetheless. It's fair enough to see this as an absurd and thankless task. That's one view, but here's mine: if you're going to speak *at all*, you must understand, and be comfortable with, the fact that *sometimes you will be wrong*. There's just no other way. And writing a column—writing *on the run*—means being comfortable with the fact that you will sometimes be wrong in front of a whole hell of a lot of people.

In this book, I have collected forty-eight of my columns that appeared in the *Toronto Star* from September 2016 to the present day that test, for me, this exact ability. And I have organized them into six parts covering six broad themes:

- **Civil Liberties and Human Rights** focuses on LGBTQ2S+ rights and broader social justice topics.
- **Portraits of Leadership** examines the worlds of both business and politics to ask what constitutes effective leadership.
- **In Power** explores the politics and perils of governing, covering predominantly—though not exclusively—the Wynne Liberals and Ford Conservatives in Ontario and the Trudeau Liberals in Ottawa.
- **In Opposition** probes the nature of effective opposition, offering insight on the task of holding government to account.
- **The Trump Years** grapples with the impact of the infamous forty-fifth president of the United States, from his battle to become the Republican nominee to the waning years of his mandate.
- **The COVID-19 Crisis** assesses the realpolitik of the COVID-19 pandemic, the leaders and institutions that rose to the challenge, and those that crumbled before the crisis.

Each part includes an introduction to the key themes and ideas covered in the selected columns. Importantly, the columns are not simply those I believe stand up best in the light of contemporary judgment or sensibilities, nor do they represent my safest opinions. Rather, I have deliberately sought out my most egregious misses.

Therefore, after each column, I've included a short commentary. These entries are a reflective exercise: with the benefit of hindsight, I examine what I got right and wrong, and offer what *I wish I'd said*, be it something entirely different, moderately adjusted, or expressed much more forcefully.

So that you can know what I think of my past work straightaway and where I'll be headed in my reflection, each commentary features one of the three following symbols:

- The "**thumbs up**" represents those columns where I got it right.

- The "**thought bubble**" represents those columns where I came close but didn't quite hit the mark.

- The "**thumbs down**" represents my undeniable misses.

With my comments, one might say I'm taking revenge on one of column writing's primary restraints—the imposition of that four p.m. Friday deadline. Therefore, in an effort to play fair, I've reserved a column's other greatest restraint: length, restricting myself to commentaries of no more than 350 words (approximately half the length of a traditional column).

- 350 words to set the record straight.
- 350 words to admonish my past opinions and beliefs.
- 350 words to offer new ones.

And in writing those 350 words, I have come to better understand not only myself and my beliefs but also how and why I came to form them. I am now better acquainted with both my bad instincts and my good ones. I'm aware of the quality of the temptation that took me down false paths, and equally of the dazzling nature of those beliefs proven to be fruitful and correct.

I very much hope this collection repeats what those original columns aspired to do: to arouse conversation and debate, to amuse and stimulate.

More importantly, I hope this book serves as a kind of challenge to all of us to reflect on our beliefs—the old ones and the new. That the columns, set against my new commentaries, inspire you to ask not only what you wish you'd said but also to consider more closely and carefully what you're going to say next.

1

Civil Liberties and Human Rights

The Freedom to Express

The greatest joy of being a columnist is that no one tells you what to write. No editor assigns you a story to cover. You get to write about whatever you want. It's kind of like being a tenured professor—except, dare I say, more people read what you produce.

And while there are times you struggle to find something fresh to say, that challenge is nothing compared to the incredible joy and privilege a perch in Speakers' Corner affords.

For me, that soapbox is especially valuable when writing about civil liberties and human rights.

The fight for equality for LGBTQ2S+ people has been the defining fight of my life. From employment benefits for our partners to equal marriage, it has been a long, at times frustrating, but ultimately exhilarating effort.*

---

* I'll be employing the term "LGBTQ2S+" consistently throughout this book, even though this term might not have appeared in my original columns. I use this inclusive acronym today to honour the members of my community, whether lesbian, gay, bisexual, trans, questioning, Two-Spirit, or those who in any capacity find themselves under the umbrella.

It is a fight that has deepened my understanding about the intersectionality of many of these issues. It's also a topic that I've not been shy about using the privilege of my column to write about—even if it means that there's a tsunami of hate mail every time I do.

Compared to writing about the ins and outs of, say, electoral politics, these subjects always elicit, to be polite, a stronger response. I regularly get three-to-four-thousand-word tirades, to which I send the same standard form response:

> Thank you for your thoughtful comments.
>
> Next time you find this much time on your hands on a Sunday afternoon, perhaps you might instead drive someone to a chemotherapy appointment, read to the blind, or bake a pie for an infirm neighbour.
>
> Very best,
> JSW

And with that, they are never heard from again!

These columns, after all, are a conspicuous target for people's feelings. Of course, these feelings are weightier than those related to the other political topics I regularly write about. They cut deeper to the bone because they're about people's sense of *who they are*.

Writing on these subjects quickly teaches you that there is *always* someone with a greater connection or lived experience, with more at stake. The nature of opinion writing—the space you are afforded and the time pressures fundamental to it—means it's impossible to reflect all experiences and views adequately. Sadly, it also means that you will inevitably do some of those experiences and views injustice.

So, often, it was with these columns that the "I wish I'd said" feeling did not dawn on me all these years later, but rather *right away*.

These columns also offer a window into Canada's diversity. Much as some might wish, conceptions of liberties and rights are neither stable, nor are they universally held. This, of course, makes wading into the debate all the more fraught. But the juice is worth the squeeze because the prize is knowing that you've made a real difference: changed people's minds or, at the very least, challenged their beliefs on the ideas that matter most.

Significantly, these rewards are not a given; they do not derive from simply having taken the risk to chime in on a controversial topic, rather—in my experience—they depend on a column achieving three things.

First, it must discuss matters with immediate, real-life relevance to people's lives. Forget fanciful and hypothetical issues. The academy can take care of theory; columnists should focus on practical concerns.

Second, on a related front, the column must deal with local issues. In my case, for the most part that means Canadian issues. So, while I frequently comment on topics that arise in the US, I strive to bring the conversation back to a uniquely Canadian context.* Given our astonishingly enriching diversity, that frequently involves drawing firm lines in the sand. Lines that make clear that no cultural or religious traditions override the inalienable rights and freedoms afforded all our citizens by the Canadian Charter, with particular care extended to people of historically marginalized communities.

Third, the column must advance a fresh perspective. (Trust me, this is especially hard when you write a column on Friday that's not published until Sunday, and everyone has been writing about the topic since Monday!)

So when I turned my pen to subjects of civil liberties and human rights, it was with these three objectives in mind. Yet I also aimed to discuss these challenging issues by reflecting them through my personal lens. Specifically, based on my experience as a gay man in the struggle for equal rights, I tried to offer my opinion on how to build change that will endure. There is an aphorism that generals always fight the last war—meaning that we tend to reuse the strategies that have worked for us in the past. To build durable change, activists must realize that the tactics that persuaded hearts and minds to a cause in one instance won't necessarily work again. For too many, that can be a painful lesson to learn.

---

* The exception to my focus on Canadian issues is, no doubt, when I write about Trump. I dedicated a section of this book to him for three reasons. One, he is endlessly fascinating. Two, readers can't get enough of him. Three, I can't take my eyes off him and his impact on American democracy.

Many people, I know, feel pessimistic about our current state of affairs. In these next columns, I cover issues where our failures to improve and protect the lives of the most vulnerable among us give rise to feelings of deep distress. From the fentanyl crisis to welcoming refugees from Afghanistan, we must do better. But while these issues will continue to challenge us, this exercise, this section, mostly gives me great hope. I am reminded that column writing is, in itself, a remarkable example of my right to free expression.

Would a hypothetical fascist government chop off my head for what I've said in the following columns? God, I hope so.

May 21, 2017

As was the case with AIDS, many people believe fentanyl will never be an issue for them personally. But it's becoming clear fentanyl is an issue that will affect all Canadians.

Fentanyl Crisis Echoes Mistakes of HIV/AIDS Response

Abuse of fentanyl, the highly addictive opioid pain medication, is taking a menacing toll across Canada.

Opioid-related overdoses killed 1,400 Canadians last year. To label the situation a coast-to-coast crisis is a massive understatement.

Fentanyl can be found in knock-off prescription painkillers, in party drugs, and even in cocaine.

The fact that other drugs are being laced with fentanyl means that drug users often haven't actively sought out the "thrill" of fentanyl and don't even realize what they've done until it's too late.

My firm, Navigator, has recently conducted a nationwide survey on public opinion relating to the fentanyl crisis in Canada.

Today, only half of Canadians say they are familiar with fentanyl-related issues. What's more troubling is that those most vulnerable, those aged sixteen to seventeen, are least familiar. Only four in ten teens are aware of the crisis.

The impact has, to date, been uneven across our country and so, therefore, has awareness. For example, 70 percent of British Columbians express awareness compared to only 49 percent of Torontonians.

The fentanyl crisis has spread so quickly, the public hardly noticed it was happening. Government officials didn't notice it either. As a result, it went largely unaddressed. And as so often happens, issues affecting the poorest or most vulnerable among us are the last to be noticed. It has only been as the crisis has transcended class lines and begun affecting suburban teenagers that the outcry has begun.

Also, problematically and mistakenly, the fentanyl issue has been seen primarily as a matter of criminal justice.

If it is to be dealt with successfully, it must be seen as a matter of public health. In a hospital, a person who dulls their pain with fentanyl is a patient. On the street, that same person is a criminal.

Fortunately, the current federal government has broken with its predecessor on this issue, and we are starting to make progress in treating the fentanyl crisis as the public health crisis it is.

Perhaps the biggest challenge has been that the public at large has not felt, so far, that the fentanyl crisis affects them. They continue to believe it is a problem faced by addicts and drug abusers who rely on illegal substances. There has been little public sympathy, and many people perceive fentanyl to be of little risk to them, far removed from everyday life.

It is a situation that has striking parallels to the HIV/AIDS crisis of the 1980s and 1990s, an indelibly tragic mark on Western society's record of compassion.

The existence of a life-threatening public health crisis that has no prevention plan in place would usually cause moral outrage. The outbreak of SARS and H1N1 both saw heightened government action, panicked media coverage, and widespread agreement to address the issues.

But, in both the HIV/AIDS and fentanyl crises, the general population has viewed the victims as foreign. HIV/AIDS was long dismissed as a gay disease, a consequence of living an immoral lifestyle.

Action was taken only once those ostensibly "moral" judgments were challenged.

Far too many people died an unnecessary death. Western nations sat idly by as a crisis ravaged a class of people they did not deem to be important enough, or moral enough, to be worth saving. Famously, President Ronald Reagan never even uttered the words "HIV" or "AIDS," even at the height of the pandemic.

A similar crisis is developing around fentanyl. Drugs are seen as taboo by large segments of the population, and drug laws provoke passionate political responses.

As was the case with AIDS, many people believe fentanyl will never be an issue for them personally. In public-policy debates, the well-being of drug addicts is rarely of prime consideration.

But it's becoming clear fentanyl is an issue that will affect all Canadians.

Moving forward, the issue requires immediate and formal co-operation among government agencies, law enforcement groups, elected officials at all levels, the emergency management infrastructure, educators, civil society, parents, and families.

It is simply not enough to sit idly by while the most vulnerable among us die of a preventable situation. This is not the first time we have found ourselves in such circumstances and we must be vigilant that it does not happen again.

The fentanyl crisis, an insidious one, threatens to undermine the lessons we learned from health crises of the past.

Canada can, and must, do better.

Since writing this column, pathetically little has changed. Indeed, evidence suggesting fentanyl represents a public health emergency has—sadly but predictably—only grown stronger. Government figures show a total of 34,455 apparent opioid toxicity deaths in Canada between 2016 and 2022, a large percentage of which involve fentanyl or fentanyl analogues. In under six years, 34,455 people.[1] That's about the size of Stratford, Ontario. And COVID-19 just exacerbated the crisis.

But I'd like to further examine the psychological and ethical dimensions at play.

Near the middle of the piece, I state that a person who dulls their pain with street fentanyl is considered a criminal while someone who does the same while hospitalized is a patient. In our society, the line between behaviours that justify an individual's stay in a hospital room versus a jail cell is very thin. And as the AIDS crisis revealed, where that line falls is often highly prejudiced.

So, what I'm most interested in today is revisiting my idea of people ignoring problems that do not directly impact their own lives. Denialism as a defence mechanism reappears throughout this section and in the wider book. For example, we eventually learned that COVID-19 (deemed by xenophobes the "Wuhan flu") would impact *everyone,* yet many bigots used it as a pretext to spew hate. Remember Vancouver in 2020? Anti-Asian hate crimes rose 717 percent there.[2] Unfortunately, it's a story we saw all across Canada.

For some, it's far easier to believe that HIV/AIDS is only a risk to "immoral" gay men or that fentanyl is only a threat to criminals and drug addicts than face uncomfortable facts. So, while I declare that it is "not enough to sit idly by while the most vulnerable among us die of a preventable situation," here is the uncomfortable truth I didn't tackle: some people amongst us simply *do* prefer to sit idly by. Nothing short of a social problem that *directly* impacts their lives can force them to act. It is a sad, disturbing truth, but one I ultimately should have raised.

October 15, 2018

*Canada has branded itself as humanitarian, but other smaller countries
are leaving us in the dust with actions, not just words.*

It Is Time to Polish Our Humanitarian Brand in Canada

I n an age of social media and intense global competition, "brand" has
become more important than ever. While it was once the exclusive
domain of consumer-focused companies, now individuals, organizations, and nations alike have become acutely aware of the image they project
and the benefits that come with successfully building brand equity.

Whatever you may be selling, branding is the alchemy that transforms
a kernel of truth and a dash of exaggeration into gold.

Intellectually, we all understand that a certain toothpaste will not transform our social lives, but on a crowded shelf the brand that's promoted will
still be the one we reach for.

The same phenomenon applies to countries. Branding has become an
important way to promote that same shelf appeal, to attract foreign capital,
top talent, jobs and corporate offices, and tourists. If you happen to have a
jaunty red maple leaf as a national logo, all the better.

The Trudeau Liberals have been, since their election, exceptionally
savvy about national and international branding. They shrewdly played to
the deep-rooted belief among Canadian voters that we are a kinder, gentler,
and more moral society than many others. They championed environmental

standards, they spoke fervently about human rights, they pronounced on the imperative for gender equality.

Not only that, they generously gave other countries pointers on how to hold themselves to that Canadian standard of conduct.

One of the most obvious examples of that moral brand extension came in August when Foreign Minister Chrystia Freeland used Twitter—in Arabic—to support Saudi activists at odds with the ruling monarchy. As tensions grew, the Canadian ambassador was withdrawn. Public demands by the Saudis for an apology were made and rejected. And the Liberals burnished Canada's brand as a plucky and high-minded nation that punched above its weight.

All that has come to the fore again, as the mystery surrounding the disappearance of a Saudi journalist—and critic of the monarchy—has deepened. On October 2, Jamal Khashoggi entered the Saudi embassy in Istanbul to complete some routine paperwork. He has not been seen since.

The international concern about his fate and the outrage at the likelihood that he is a victim of dire retribution has certainly vindicated Canada's early stand against an increasingly bold autocracy.

But here's where the varnish starts to chip: the values that underpin our national brand are not consistent with finger-wagging diplomacy and impassioned rhetoric about the importance of human rights.

Indeed, our own sense of our brand is at odds with reality—and with the perceptions of others. When the Canadian government—first the Conservatives and then the Liberals—agreed to sell armoured vehicles to Saudi Arabia, they unequivocally forfeited the moral high ground. Sure, they were described first as "trucks" by former prime minister Stephen Harper and later as "Jeeps" by Prime Minister Justin Trudeau, but that deliberate trivialization only makes it worse. The Saudis know that perfectly well and, frankly, so does everyone else.

This is not going to be a one-time news story. Rather, it is going to be an issue as Canada's campaign to join the 2021 UN Security Council ramps up. The effort is already underway, skilfully led by Canada's permanent representative to the United Nations, Marc-André Blanchard. Given our sense of our own brand, Canada should be a strong contender. But remember what happened last time we tried for this prize. Portugal left us in their dust.

And now, we're competing for a coveted spot with Norway and Ireland, two smaller and quieter countries with less brand equity but perhaps more authentic clout. For all our posturing, the reality is that Norway is a far more generous foreign-aid donor (spending one percent of GDP compared with Canada's 0.26 percent), and Ireland has twice as many peacekeepers in the field as Canada.

Just another example of the complexities that middle powers face when trying to give life to their brand and their values in a big, old, complicated, and cross-pressured world.

Well, it turns out that the Trudeau government's actions, which blatantly contradicted the branding of the kind, gentle, and moral Canada they helped facilitate and advance did, in fact, hurt our country's standing in the bid to join the UN Security Council. I got that right. Despite costly diplomatic efforts, Canada fell short to Norway and Ireland—an embarrassing moment in which we lost our bid for the coveted seat that would've bolstered our international standing and signalled Canada's capacity to punch above its weight when it comes to global peacekeeping and security.[3]

But I went wrong by deeming the Liberals' efforts "savvy." Even *more dangerous* than the absence of effective branding is branding that is false or disingenuous.

Let me explain. In assisting clients through a crisis, I often tell them that authenticity and integrity matter above all. Why? Because Canadians are reasonable people. They understand that mistakes happen. That said, they know bad behaviour when they see it. And there is perhaps no worse behaviour than purposeful deceit. Canada's posturing on the international stage fits this description.

This lesson in authenticity applies to the world of branding in several important respects. If you have a strong brand, there's an extent to which it can protect you against minor issues or contradictions. If, however, a brand is *proven* to be untrue, or worse, misleading—then the damage can be ruinous. In short, the pain is worse when someone you know and trust lets you down, versus someone you don't. This is the considerable gamble the Trudeau government made. Unfortunately, they lost.

But, in the end, the new security reality brought on by the war in Ukraine has fundamentally changed the calculus of Canada's brand on the global stage and provides an exit ramp for the Liberals' misguided branding efforts. No longer can we pretend to own any moral high ground. We are a middle power who must play our role to support our NATO allies. Anything more, once again, risks perilous contradiction.

October 13, 2019

Having reached her eighth decade, my mother lives in a country almost unique in the world where there are no restrictions on her ability to vote regardless of how much her mental condition deteriorates.

Safeguarding the Right to Vote for All Citizens, Regardless of Age

As we all gathered around to celebrate Thanksgiving this weekend, I felt especially grateful for my incredible family and so lucky to have with us my amazing mother, a woman whose view of the world and commitment to the service of others has so profoundly influenced me and the person I have become.

Sadly, in recent years, my mother's cognitive facilities have declined with a swiftness that is both devastating and unspeakably heartbreaking.

As our family, like so many others, talked about the election together this weekend, I began to think about the role played by Canadians—approximately five hundred thousand Canadians—with cognitive impairments in our most basic democratic tradition. How, I wondered, do individuals like my mother participate in our democracy and what supports are in place for them to do so?

By the next election in 2023-2024, nearly one in five Canadians will be older than sixty-five, and with that demographic shift will come increased rates of Alzheimer's and dementia. We also know that older voters turn out to the polls in disproportionate numbers.

Having reached her eighth decade, my mother lives in a country almost unique in the world where there are no restrictions on her ability to vote regardless of how much her mental condition deteriorates. In a survey of sixty-two countries, only four lacked a mental-capacity requirement on the right to vote. (The others are Ireland, Italy, and Sweden.) Within Canada, only one province or territory, Nunavut, has such a restriction on the eligibility to vote.

South of the border, by contrast, such restrictions are the norm. More than thirty US states have laws limiting those with mental disabilities or cognitive impairments from voting if they have been ruled legally incompetent.

These restrictions do not only impact the elderly, as many illnesses or conditions can result in cognitive impairment, including multiple sclerosis, strokes, traumatic brain injuries, Parkinson's or Huntington's disease, as well as Alzheimer's and dementia. In cases where successful legal challenges have been mounted against mental-capacity requirements, the plaintiffs are often autistic.

As with so many of the battles over voting rights, the argument in favour of restrictions boils down to a defence against voter fraud. Proponents fear that people will use the vulnerable and the elderly to harvest their ballots.

Until 1993, this was the basis of the law in Canada, as dictated by the mental-capacity provision of the Canada Elections Act, which excluded from voting any person who was "restrained of his liberty of movement or deprived of the management of his property by reason of mental disease." That year, Madam Justice Reed held that the provision was in violation of the Charter, which guarantees to every Canadian citizen the right to vote.

"It simply does not follow that people who are declared incapable of managing their financial affairs are necessarily incapable of understanding the nature of the right to vote and of exercising it in a rational manner," wrote Justice Reed.

While subsequent blue-ribbon panels recommended a narrower restriction, Parliament opted simply to repeal the law in time for the 1993 federal election.[4] Nothing has yet replaced it, and so far, our democracy has got along just fine since then.

What's more, a number of informal approaches have developed to ensure abuse does not take place. US surveys have shown that in nursing homes, where this kind of challenge is a perennial problem, staff have figured out a gatekeeping system, quizzing residents on political questions to assess whether they are in a state of mind to vote.

The approach that forbids anyone in a long-term care home or anyone with a cognitive impairment from voting is rooted in an outdated view of mental health. Where once we sought to institutionalize those with mental disabilities to be cared for and saved from themselves, today, the prevailing view favours integration with the community. Today, the goal is a meaningful life lived as much as possible like everyone else. And there is no more meaningful contribution to our society than voting.

That's why, on October 21, I will be proud to help my mother vote. For the person she thinks is best suited to be her MP.

SHOULD HAVE DIVED DEEPER

Since I wrote this column, the amazing woman I describe—who gave me *everything*—has sadly passed away. This column is part of my tribute to her.

Though I agree with my decision to celebrate Canada's absence of mental-capacity restrictions on voting, I should've both asked and attempted to answer corresponding questions in two key areas.

The first concerns the practical support necessary to ensure all citizens are able to cast their vote. The COVID-19 pandemic generated new barriers to voting for the elderly and those who live with visible and invisible disabilities. While the various independent provincial agencies and Elections Canada did an admirable job, the fact remains that throughout the pandemic, we saw horrifically low voter turnout. It's incumbent upon us to entertain the following thought: What if we are hit by a disease *more* infectious and deadlier than COVID-19? What practical supports would be needed then? What if we are forced, not simply to use voting machines, but to vote fully online? What infrastructure would be required then to guarantee the integrity and accessibility of our elections? And why, parenthetically, have we not got that sorted out now?

Second, I should have explored our changing demographic. Canada is getting older. Not just by a little, but by *a lot*. And with this fact, beyond the matter of elderly people's right to vote, there are important political dynamics at play. The often unsaid sentiment sometimes expressed by younger generations is, crudely put, why should those who won't be around for long get to decide what impacts the lives of those who will? The venomous prejudice of ageism is rooted in such a question. The cruel and obvious subtext? Elderly voices and lives matter less because they are closer to death.

Here's the core issue: this poison will only spread further as the generational divide expands. As a country, we need to stay on top of this. The first steps to combatting it are, surely, calling out such bigotry at the moment it arises and doing everything we can to prevent ageism and ableism from infecting our politics.

June 6, 2020

It is not my place to say what the demands of the (anti-Black racism)
protestors should be or what shape the movement should take next,
but I feel it would be a tragedy to move away from the basis
of the movement in protest.

Protest Is a Powerful Force for Progress

In January 1909, a group of notable Americans signed their names to a statement that called for a national conference focused on the civil and political rights of Black Americans. The "Call" was signed by the likes of W. E. B. Dubois and Ida B. Wells, and it contended that the upcoming centenary of Abraham Lincoln's birth should be a day of "taking stock of the nation's progress since 1865."

"How far has [the nation] lived up to the obligations imposed upon it by the Emancipation Proclamation? How far has it gone in assuring to each and every citizen, irrespective of colour, the equality of opportunity, and equality before the law, which underlie our American institutions and are guaranteed by the Constitution?" asked the letter.

The unfortunate answer, affirmed over a century later by the voices of thousands of Americans this past week, is clear: nowhere near far enough.

Many signatories of the "Call" would go on to form the NAACP, officially established just a few weeks later. In its 111-year history, the NAACP evolved from a relatively small association focused on litigation against Jim Crow laws, into a national organization with half a million members and tangible political power.

Like many civil rights organizations, it was born from emotion, specifically anger, frustration, and disappointment in the deferred promise of 1865 (the passage of the Thirteenth Amendment). But over the years, civil rights leaders like Dubois and Wells channelled that emotion into positive action, without which the United States would be less free, less equal, and less just a society than it is today.

As protests spread this week across the United States and here at home—protests that have jolted so many of us out of our privileged complacency—it's important to remember the legacy of civil rights organizations and their roots in protest.

The simple fact is that direct action works: from the civil rights movement of the mid-twentieth century to the Stonewall riots and the origins of Pride, protest and civil unrest have long served as catalysts for important change. The protests surrounding the murder of George Floyd at the hands of Minneapolis police are no different.

Consider just how much the Black Lives Matter movement has evolved since its inception in 2013. What began as a hashtag has grown into an international phenomenon, the animating spirit of the largest protests seen in nearly fifty years. While its actions were once the subject of controversy, corporations and brands now eagerly endorse its message.

Along the way, Black Lives Matter has remained steadfastly committed to its roots as a protest movement. Local chapters of the movement have now, for seven years, led protests in response to far too many deaths, all too similar to George Floyd's. With each action, the loose network envisioned by the movement's founders has grown stronger.

The natural question to ask next is what happens to the Black Lives Matter movement from here? Perhaps the movement will go the way of Pride: corporatized and mainstream, far now from its roots in protest. Like Pride, victory here may not ultimately mean a set of policy changes so much as a shifting of the Overton window—a victory of the public sense of what's possible and expected.

But regardless of where the movement ultimately goes, this is coming to a head. We are experiencing a once-in-a-generation paroxysm about the health and safety of Black communities, prompted by both the coronavirus and the latest instances of police brutality.

It is not my place to say what the demands of the protestors should be or what shape the movement should take next, but I feel it would be a tragedy to move away from the basis of the movement in protest.

After all, we have seen, again and again, how the courage and leadership of organizers and protestors alike have sustained the movement through years of growth.

That said, any meaningful, sustainable change that comes next will depend on all of us—how our expectations, our behaviour, and our attitudes evolve. And that means, first and foremost, looking inward and addressing, in the words of James Baldwin, the "many things we do not wish to know about ourselves."

Since I wrote this column in June 2020, the power of protest has, evidently, gone nowhere. Today, I'd make two additional comments.

The first stems from my experience fighting for gay rights across multiple decades. To validate a movement's "basis in protest" is to characterize its early days by its participants' energy, motivation, aversion to the status quo, and willingness to test new ideas. These are the qualities that motivate people to "vote with their feet" or launch online protests. Qualities that must be protected but too often fade away.

This isn't to say that Pride or any other movement that has courted and enjoyed corporate backing is somehow impure or uninspiring. Such actions are simply part of expanding the movement. But this needs to be done with enormous care. If the movement grows strong enough, it can actually *change* corporations themselves. But when a movement loses sight of its principles, cynicism can make even those who once believed in the cause lose faith in the possibility of change.

The second observation flows from my experience advising businesses and political leaders across Canada on a variety of issues that, in some cases, have been burbling beneath the surface for years—#MeToo, Time's Up, Idle No More.

These movements illustrate that widespread protests don't arise spontaneously. Certainly, there are instigating actions—as in the case of George Floyd's murder. But pay close attention to your constituents, customers, or stakeholders and you may see these issues coming. Then, it's up to you to act.

The first step? Deciding whether to be an active supporter or to remain on the sidelines. Throughout my career, I have seen governments and businesses destroy their reputation by failing to plan strategically and issuing ill-advised, thoughtless responses to a new movement or protest, producing rushed and transparently inauthentic messaging. But unjustifiably withholding support can leave them wholly unprepared for the predictable backlash and media firestorm.

It's impossible to get everything right. That said, a bit of forethought will allow you to get as much right as you possibly can.

February 14, 2021

Facebook's algorithms and business model have long preferred divisive and extreme content over peer-to-peer interaction or reliable news sources. As long as users continue to prefer the sort of content that has wrought so much havoc, don't expect any serious change.

Purging Political Content from Facebook, Zuckerberg Is a Modern-Day Pandora

This week, Mark Zuckerberg announced that Facebook will test changes to its algorithm to cut back the political content on its network and rein in divisiveness. The move is welcome news for those who recognize the corrosive influence of the platform on political discourse and who are aghast at its real-life consequences.

Canada, alongside Brazil and Indonesia, will be the sandbox for this shift.

Perhaps we should feel lucky. Somehow, I doubt it.

That's because this decision reveals Zuckerberg to be no more than a modern-day Pandora, attempting to recapture the ills and monsters he has previously released from the box. For years, his company has encouraged division and radical politics, along the way realizing just how popular and profitable it can be. Over time, Facebook's users have been rewired to seek out disagreement and extremes, rather than the connections and shared values of friends and family.

So, it's no surprise that Facebook's platform has become something very different from the social network it set out to create.

For those who have been paying attention, like *New York Times* tech columnist Kevin Roose, this shift has been a long time coming. If Zuckerberg is Pandora, then consider Roose our Cassandra, another heroine of Greek mythology who was cursed with the power of tragic prophecies doomed to be ignored by all.

Over the summer, Roose began tracking the top-performing link posts on US Facebook, sharing the top ten via his Twitter account. This list was a consistent revolving door of heavily biased news outlets and political agitators like Ben Shapiro, Franklin Graham, and Breitbart News. It captured, in real time, the degradation of discourse on Facebook. Given the world's largest social network is also a primary source of news for millions of North Americans, this is an alarming trend.

To be clear, it's no accident that these are the top performers. For too long, Facebook's algorithms—and indeed its business model—have preferred divisive and extreme content over peer-to-peer interaction or reliable news sources.

So, while some argue that Facebook is addressing the root of the issue by focusing on the algorithms that got it into this mess in the first place, I disagree. Facebook's algorithms will always be geared toward the ultimate purpose of more engagement, greater profits, and wider use. Sadly, that purpose is best served by content that feeds us what we've been taught to desire: self-affirming perspectives and extreme opinions.

When Facebook's desire to moderate that content comes in conflict with its bottom line, the company's true colours are revealed.

After the presidential election, Facebook modified its algorithm to prioritize trustworthy, respected news sources in order to curtail misinformation about election fraud and stopping "the steal." The encouraging move left many to wonder if it would be permanently implemented to clean up the site and turn down the temperature.

Unfortunately, the move was temporary. This and similar changes to the algorithm had to be canned when it became clear they would not only calm divisions but also reduce user engagement. At Facebook, profit trumps any desire to clean up the platform. And as long as users continue to prefer exactly the sort of content that has wrought so much havoc on our civil society and our politics, don't expect any serious change.

The cynical view is that Facebook is simply blowing smoke to avoid intervention by the new Biden administration's tech skeptics. Biden himself admitted in a January interview that he's "never been a fan of Facebook" or of Zuckerberg. Many Facebook hawks within the Federal Trade Commission and elsewhere believe the new administration is their opportunity to finally go after what they see as a flagrant violation of antitrust laws.

But Zuckerberg also faces pressure from within. In November, Buzzfeed reported widespread disillusionment among Facebook employees—only 51 percent of whom said they believed the company has a positive impact on the world. That's a massive problem in a sector as competitive as tech.[5]

So, before we congratulate Zuckerberg for this change, let's consider the motives behind it. More importantly, let's see if it sticks or, for that matter, if it makes a difference.

Mark Zuckerberg. Remember him?

While Facebook's (now Meta) famously robotic CEO might've faded somewhat from public consciousness, issues with tech algorithms, especially those of social media companies, have gone nowhere. In fact, they've only worsened (or, to the tech overlords, *improved*) since I wrote this column in early 2021. As new platforms emerge globally, it has become clear that I shouldn't have limited my prediction to Facebook. Almost all of these platforms are, at the end of the day, businesses, and will always be driven by profit first. As long as controversy and divisiveness drive the most engagement, that is precisely what the algorithms will prioritize.

How are politicians to deal with this issue? To my mind, there are two options. Option one is increased regulation: If governments want to rein in extremism on these platforms, would it not be most efficient to regulate what these algorithms can search and prioritize? While it sounds appealing in concept, in practice, this would be difficult to execute. Logistically, it would be an impossible challenge for one national government to control what is said on global social media websites. Moreover, the idea of one entity controlling all of mass media is disturbing. If a government were to have a particularly harmful opinion about, say, LGBTQ2S+ rights, would it not be better to have independent social media capable of challenging its views? We have seen these fears manifest with the vocal protests surrounding Bills C-11[6] and C-18.[7] Neither piece of legislation is nearly as restrictive as what's suggested above, yet resistance has been fierce. Therefore, to me at least, option one is not a realistic fix.

Option two is far simpler: go with the flow. If social media companies are going to continue to highlight controversial posts that drive engagement, then perhaps it is best to follow suit. Many successful politicians have used this strategy to their advantage: Jagmeet Singh, Pierre Poilievre and, infamously, Donald Trump all come to mind. Social media is a modern retelling of an old political truth rather than an entirely new lesson for politicians. You either adapt or die.

June 6, 2021

Canadian activists needed the courts to enshrine LGBTQ2S+ rights, and yes, a great effort was made to win over the hearts and minds of Canadians. But ultimately, once the LGBTQ2S+ community was able to transform our struggle into a charter fight, the battle was won.

This Pride Month Evokes the Tension Between Battles for Legal Rights and Public Recognition—For Canadians, that History Is Unique

Happy Pride. It's become a refrain you'll hear again and again this month—from colleagues, friends, family, your favourite sports team, your bank, your dentist . . .

Indeed, Pride, and the deluge of rainbow ribbons that arrives with it, has become the event of the season for corporate Canada.

Most would agree that the rush of brands to wrap themselves in the rainbow flag for the month of June is both symbolically and practically important.

And despite its faults—it has been decried as virtue signalling, or worse, "pinkwashing"—I will happily take even performative displays of LGTBQ2S+ support over the alternative: deafening silence.

That is especially true this year, when so much seems so uncertain. In Canada, the vestiges of institutional homophobia have reared their heads as the government rushes to ban conversion therapy and faces pressure to end the discriminatory blood ban. Meanwhile, Republican lawmakers in the US have recently descended into a politically vacuous and morally reprehensible fixation on trans rights.

And before the month is out, the US Supreme Court will deliver its ruling in a case with important implications for LGBTQ2S+ rights: Fulton v. City of Philadelphia. The case, which hinges on whether religiously affiliated foster-care agencies are entitled to turn away same-sex couples, may have a disappointing outcome.

Legislative battles that emerge from embers. Court challenges that spring from the fertile minds of lawyers. Homophobic responses rooted in everyday life. Reminders all of the work that remains to be done.

Over the decades, there has always been strong tension within the LGBTQ2S+ community around how to win the fight for equality, with much of that argument coming down to the proverbial question about the chicken or the egg.

Some believed that we had to first win the battle for the hearts and minds of our family and friends, now fashionably called "allies," before we could hope to get the laws changed.

Others believed Martin Luther King Jr. when he said, "It may be true that the law cannot change the heart, but it can restrain the heartless." These people believed it was essential to win in the courts first.

Today, it is obvious that these two approaches, more than not being mutually exclusive, are in fact mutually dependent.

In the pre-Stonewall era of the 1960s, the fight for equality hinged on recognition as a "respectable" minority that could assimilate into the establishment. LGBTQ2S+ leaders emphasized propriety in the public eye and quiet recognition in the courts.

Then came Stonewall, and shortly thereafter, the Pride parades we know today. Singular moments when the focus shifted toward public recognition and visibility. In the United States, that shift came before the eventual legal victories, wherein the rights of LGBTQ2S+ Americans were affirmed by the Supreme Court.

In Canada, the story is somewhat different; the distinctions in our own fight for equality mimic the nuances of our system. That's largely because of our Charter of Rights and Freedoms and the fact that—despite the grumbling of certain politicians—Canadians *are* a people of the Charter.

True, Canadian activists needed the courts to enshrine LGBTQ2S+ rights, and yes, a great effort was made to win over the hearts and minds of Canadians.

But ultimately, once the LGBTQ2S+ community was able to transform our fight into a charter fight, the battle was won. By wrapping our fight in the Charter, Canadians could see that it was also their fight—that a threat to any Charter protection was a threat to all Canadians.

And so, the tension between public advocacy and legal recognition, which was unique in Canada, provided the most precious of results. It provided us a country where—while law has given us equality—the people have given us true and genuine inclusiveness.

An inclusiveness which will not soon disappear. An inclusiveness that, while imperfect, is still something that makes this gay man, partner, father, and grandfather a proud Canadian.

MISSED OPPORTUNITY

As much as I'm heartened by the progress this column describes, I find myself focusing primarily on the negatives. And when I look closely, I find many.

For example, despite gay men clinching the win in 2022 with the ending of the blood ban, other marginalized groups, including sex workers, continue to be discriminated against when it comes to donating blood.[8]

The US Supreme Court's ruling on Fulton v. City of Philadelphia,[9] in response to a Catholic Social Services claim that they should be allowed to decline same-sex couples for foster-care placement, could have proven to be a landmark case for LGBTQ2S+ rights but instead proved to be a minor victory for conservative religious groups, bypassing important questions regarding religious accommodations for LGBTQ2S+ folks.

These cases of ongoing discrimination underscore that much work remains to achieve inclusion and equality for all.

I should've highlighted the difference of opinion amongst gay activists. No matter how bitterly some in my community disagreed on strategy, it always felt—at least it did to me—that we were on the same team. The way the so-called "culture wars" are playing out today, I'm not so sure that's true. Many factions on the progressive left are bitterly divided. While some divisions are ideological, many are tactical. They agree they want to see climate action, trans rights, and universal basic income platformed, but they *cannot* seem to agree on how to bring it about, how soon, and by what means.

People who are fighting for the same ultimate goal *must* find a way to agree on a path forward. The American colonies would not have got very far if they hadn't eventually set aside their differences to fight for their collective independence from the British. Agreeing on a path forward toward the ultimate goal depends on listening to the perspectives of others (especially those voices from within marginalized communities), identifying shared values, and being open to compromise. And in my writing moving forward, I will continue to drive the message that all parties must focus—relentlessly—on the big picture, not the minutiae that impede progress.

January 30, 2022

Tragedy looms over thousands of journalists in Afghanistan, and the clock is ticking. As Canadians, we owe them an enormous debt.

Afghan Journalists Defended "Canadian Values"—Now Our Government Must Act to Protect Them

The fall of Kabul to the Taliban cast a long shadow across our world last August. No one felt its darkness more acutely than the many brave Afghans who supported, in one way or another, the work of Western nations in their country.

Afghan journalists were among those who made an outsized contribution. Reporting on the ground—right up until the fall of Kabul on August 15—and supporting outlets from Western countries like Canada, they played the most visible of roles and, in doing so, put themselves at extreme risk of retaliation and torture.

As Canadians, we owe them an enormous debt. For over a decade, our country and its news outlets worked with these Afghans. They kept our journalists safe and informed, and their contributions helped define our role in the conflict. Simply put, they are heroes.

And yet, right now, tragedy looms over thousands of them. Having escaped or been forced from Afghanistan, these journalists remain stuck in temporary places of refuge in Pakistan, North Macedonia, and other "lily pad" countries.

For each of them, the clock is ticking. As their temporary visas expire or death threats metastasize into real, imminent danger, their situations will become dire in a matter of weeks.

Reasonably, they have turned to Canada for support and for a chance to seek refuge in a country that owes them so much. Thus far, we have failed them.

For assorted reasons, the Trudeau government and its representatives recognize this as a vexing situation. Immigration is a difficult file at the best of times, they say. Compounded by a crisis like Afghanistan, it is rife with complexity and practical hurdles.

We have heard the same arguments repeated over again:

Processing visas for this group is nearly impossible. There is an overwhelming demand for spaces in our country. We cannot get funds or support to them in terror-prone regions like Pakistan without circumventing international rules.

That may all be true, but it is high time for the government to look past these issues and act with the conviction and compassion every decent Canadian expects.

After all, these same roadblocks faced governments in the US and the UK, yet both countries have already found workarounds to carve out unique visa programs for Afghan journalists. Pathetically, Canada has not.

Instead, the government has thrown the mantle to a series of NGOs, veterans' organizations, and private charities.

These groups have done their best to step up. But the reality is, this is a job for government.

Since the pandemic began, we have seen the need for government, especially the federal government, to respond to challenges that only the public sector can address—ones that private citizens cannot.

Now, on an issue directly related to actions taken by our government, Ottawa has had the nerve to ask private organizations to step in. It is simply unacceptable.

Our federal cabinet must find the political will to get this done.

The government should earmark at least a thousand spaces specifically for journalists and their families. Failing that, they should come up with a workable solution that can be implemented in time to save hundreds of lives.

I recently heard from Shakor Kamran, a journalist forced to leave Afghanistan after reporting on Taliban abuses of power. He spoke proudly of his past work with two organizations focused on strengthening civil society by improving women's access to health care and education.

I cannot imagine a clearer reflection of what this government calls "Canadian values."

Journalists like Kamran stood up for those values, and now want the chance to live them. They most certainly have earned that chance.

And after so many years talking about Canada's gentler role on the world stage and about our support for human rights and press freedom, it is time for our government to walk the walk. These journalists can wait no longer.

MISSED THE BULLSEYE

Though it has fallen out of our mainstream discourse, thanks in no small part to Vladimir Putin's illegal invasion of Ukraine, the resettlement of Afghan journalists remains, for Canadians, a moral imperative. We *must* assist those who risked their lives to report the truth. The progress made since I penned this column in January 2022 is nowhere near enough.

In fall 2022, I attended an event where my friend Lisa LaFlamme recounted how, in reporting from Afghanistan during the conflict's early years, her Afghan translator and guide saved her life. By telling her audience about the depth of this man's courage and commitment, she brought us close to his plight and the dire circumstances he was facing after the Taliban took power. With expert skill, Lisa employed a classic journalism tactic: using one individual's story to tell a much larger story. In this column, (although I briefly touched on Kamran's experiences) I wish I'd done the same and told a better story.

Though I don't claim to have Lisa's degree of direct experience, I'd like to speak of the harrowing journey of Younus Qarizadah, a twenty-six-year-old disabled journalist now living in Pakistan. Qarizadah worked for Radio Haqiqat and Sima-e-Sulh TV in northern Afghanistan's Samangan province. His circumstances are so dire that, in February 2023, he told the *Toronto Star* he was contemplating selling his kidney in order to feed his family.

Qarizadah's story isn't an outlier, nor an exception. According to the *Toronto Star*, since the fall of Kabul, Afghanistan has lost 40 percent of its media outlets and 60 percent of its journalists, with 76 percent of its female journalists no longer working in the country. [10]

In telling Qarizadah's story today, all I would add is that Canadians can still play a vital role in improving Afghans' situation, which Afghan scholar Najim Dost likened to European rehabilitation in the post-WWII landscape. We can pressure the federal government to accept more Afghan refugees. We can donate to organizations like Journalists for Human Rights that work to evacuate vulnerable Afghans, including high-risk journalists, human rights advocates, and their family members, from Afghanistan.

May 1, 2022

The entire pathetic saga is part of a bigger push to undermine the rights of LGBTQ2S+ Americans and use their identities as a wedge issue.

America's Anti-LGBTQ2S+ Bills Are Not What They Appear to Be—Don't Look Away

For the past two weeks, Florida legislators have waged all-out war against opponents of legislation that limits discussion of LGBTQ2S+ topics in school. Many have wondered how one education bill could be worth all the trouble, but the answer is depressingly clear: this is not about a single piece of legislation in Florida. Rather, the entire pathetic saga is part of a bigger push to undermine the rights of LGBTQ2S+ Americans and use their identities as a wedge issue.

Want proof? Legislatures in twenty states from Alabama to Ohio are already moving forward with copycat legislation.

As for the law itself, I won't relitigate its details here, except to say that it is harmful, intentionally divisive and engineered to push gay, lesbian, and trans people back into the shadows.

I will, however, say how heartbroken I am to have heard so many people I know and respect parrot the many "sensible" justifications for the bill. Among them:

"Why are children in kindergarten learning about sex—*any* kind of sex?"

"The bill only bans discussion of LGBTQ2S+ topics that isn't *age appropriate.*"

"The law is meant to *protect* students from teachers."

To the first point, Florida has *already* banned sex education until Grade 5.

To the second, it's crucial to note that "age appropriate" is open to interpretation—and given that the law empowers parents to sue school boards, teachers will inevitably err on the side of caution, shutting out inclusion of LGBTQ2S+ stories and experiences.

To the third: those who present this law as an "anti-grooming bill" are simply playing to the worst tropes about gay, lesbian, and trans people. The idea that a law of this nature is necessary to protect children from predatory homosexuals is not just ridiculous, it is homophobic. It relies on a long-standing assumption that LGBTQ2S+ people are deviants. The "anti-grooming" framing also allows supporters of the bill to paint its opponents as pedophiles—the most monstrous allegation that can be made in public life.

To be clear, I don't entirely blame these people for misunderstanding the purpose of the bill; that is its framers' intent. It is intentionally vague. It uses the "parental rights" banner to usher extremely conservative, homophobic, and transphobic views into the mainstream of American politics.

And don't be fooled—while the fight began in Florida, it will not end there. There will be legal challenges to these laws in Florida and elsewhere, challenges that will work their way through a judiciary transformed by four years of Trump appointments. Eventually, one case will end up at the Supreme Court and debates about LGBTQ2S+ rights will be reopened.

This approach mirrors exactly the latest campaign against reproductive rights, which began in a small Mississippi clinic and is now before the court. It seeks to overturn Roe v. Wade, settled law for nearly fifty years.

Some say LGBTQ2S+ rights have been protected for long enough that these concerns are hysterical. But it's simply not true. Obergefell v. Hodges was decided only seven years ago, and only by a 5–4 ruling. Of those five justices, only two remain on the court today.

And we know that hate is the most powerful device of division in politics.

I was struck by a recent letter by Spencer Cox, the Republican governor of Utah, explaining his decision to veto a law that would ban transgender students from competing in girls' sport.[11]

"Here are the numbers that have most impacted my decision: 75,000, 4, 1, 86 and 56.

- Seventy-five thousand high school kids participate in high school sports in Utah.
- Four transgender kids play high school sports.
- One transgender student plays girls sports.
- Eighty-six percent of trans youth report suicidality.
- Fifty-six percent of trans youth have attempted suicide.

Four kids and only one of them playing girls sports . . . Four kids who aren't dominating or winning trophies or taking scholarships. Four kids who are just trying to find some friends and feel like they are a part of something. Four kids trying to get through each day. Rarely has so much fear and anger been directed at so few.

I don't understand what they are going through or why they feel the way they do. But I want them to live . . . I hope we can work to find ways to show these four kids that we love them, and they have a place in our state."

Cox's words are a tonic. But they also suggest a frightening admission that these laws are not actually about what they claim to be. They are about us—all LGBTQ2S+ people—and our place in society. Please don't forget that.

When I wrote this piece in the middle of 2022, it seemed that Republican lawmakers had begun a slow but determined walk down a path toward undercutting and rolling back LGBTQ2S+ rights and freedoms in the United

States. As it turns out, I was both right and wrong. Right, because I was correct that restricting LGBTQ2S+ rights is their end goal but wrong because I underestimated their speed: Republicans have acted at a breakneck pace, specifically aiming to slash the rights of transgender Americans.

Trans people have been facing near-constant attacks, both physical and legislative, in the US. Constant "protests" against drag-queen storytimes (events not unfamiliar to Canada) and a barrage of smearing and social media dogpiling have been followed up by banning hormone therapy and referring to transgender children as being "groomed." In fact, Donald Trump promised in a campaign video that, if he were to be re-elected, he would ban transgender youth from receiving gender-affirming care, which he equated to "child sex mutilation."[12]

A disgusting stance.

This shameful and aggressive display from Republicans has underscored a vital weakness in certain progressive issues that seemed to have been settled: their basis in old and vulnerable court rulings. As we have seen from the targeting of trans rights and, perhaps more decisively, the overturning of Roe v. Wade, it now seems obvious that there is no such thing as settled law. The courts can no longer be relied upon to be incorruptible bastions.

If we want to guarantee that similar issues do not occur in Canada, we must begin to codify vulnerable court rulings into law, especially those rulings on sensitive social issues like abortion. Otherwise, Canada could face a similar backslide to that of the United States, thereby threatening the lives of the ordinary citizens that the government and our country are meant to protect.

Also, trans lives matter. End of story.

2

Portraits of Leadership

Learning from the Best and the Worst

Early in my career, I had the highest privilege a young person can have: the opportunity to work alongside and get to know leaders of all kinds. To see what made them tick. To understand how they set priorities, made decisions, and how they liked their morning coffee.

And yes, just how unremarkably human they often were.

Some of those leaders were towers of strength and determination who came to their positions with a genuine desire to better the world for all of us, but especially for those less fortunate. Then there were others who didn't have a bloody clue as to why they were there or what they wanted to do—except perhaps their hair.

I had the chance to be with leaders sometimes on their first day, sometimes on their last, but many times on their very worst. You see, it is only when you stand with someone in the extreme heat of a government or personal crisis that you really get to take the measure of them. Our leaders are both revealed and tempered by crisis. And it's in those moments that we can learn everything about their character.

Later in life, I've been fortunate enough to grow to become a leader myself. As part of that growth, I have tried, in quiet moments of brutal honesty, to reflect on what I have taken from each of the leaders I've served. It's not that I set out to "take" anything. It's just that somehow, someway, their style of influence got under my skin, and I found that I could not help but to lead as they did. It's not something I lament. I see it, rather, as part of the great chain of leadership. It's simply how leaders—good and bad alike—are nurtured and developed.

So, when it comes to learning *how* to lead, there is no perfect specimen, lone exemplar, or deity after which to model oneself, much less worship. There are only flawed, humble, capricious, loving, irrational, imperfect humans.

In presenting the following columns, I have tried to reflect this wisdom. I have striven to present not creeds or doctrines of leadership but possibilities, portraits.

Yet a word of warning. I have entitled this section "Portraits of Leadership" very purposefully. Portraits are time-bound. They represent a person in a particular moment. Sometimes the light is flattering; sometimes it's harsh. The same goes for columns. While a few of the following selections are, of course, about a leader's overall legacy, most were occasioned by dramatic events: a crisis, a stunning victory, a spectacular defeat.

Of course, I would never pretend to capture a person or claim to fully know them through these mere moments in time. Portraits, like columns, never tell the full story. Still, if you wish to make progress toward understanding a leader, you must examine the actions they took in times of adversity. Every role worthy of the term "leadership" generates and shares experiences of adversity.

Leaders cannot outrun adversity. For instance, when a question is levelled against a government minister in the House of Commons, they cannot rise up and say, "Madam Speaker, please, just give me a moment to think!"

There is an old adage that you can "grow into" a leadership role. I detest this advice, though it carries a kernel of truth. A leader, after all, can and should learn and be conditioned by experience. Rather, I hate it because it sets up that false expectation that leadership is a character trait unto itself. It raises the specious idea that there is a master blueprint on successful leadership to follow—complete with a cluster of traits you can "find" or "adopt." Nonsense. Leadership roles do not transform character; they reveal character.

Here's the sad and constant truth: people with flawed personalities assume positions of leadership. While their selfishness and ego may drive them forward for a time, those same characteristics eventually drag them down. As sordid and epic as their flameouts can be, they also serve to highlight the value of positive and effective leadership, of those who keep calm and lead from the front and with integrity, no matter the circumstance. Those who, far from insulting or putting down those beneath them, lift them up.

This section of the book presents both types.

- Media mogul and philanthropist Oprah Winfrey
- The late Ottawa Centre MP for the NDP, Paul Dewar
- Former minister of justice and attorney general Jody Wilson-Raybould
- Ontario's twenty-ninth lieutenant-governor, the Honourable Elizabeth Dowdeswell
- Business executive, author, and diplomat Dominic Barton
- The Duke of York, Prince Andrew
- Former British prime minister Boris Johnson
- The current US president, Joe Biden

Nine leaders, remarkably diverse in context and style. Nine leaders who have changed the world around them. Nine leaders from whom we can learn how to lead, and how not to. Both cautionary tales and instructive ones.

I'll let you decide who I think is who.

January 14, 2018

The presidency of the United States, like all elected positions, doesn't come with training wheels. The fix to what currently ails the American presidency is not more of what injured it in the first place.

President Winfrey Has Allure, But a Celebrity Is No Solution

I t seems that with politics, just like Hollywood, what's old is new again. In Hollywood, the old ideas include *Star Wars*, *Roseanne*, *Jurassic Park*, *Jumanji* and many more.

In politics, it's Mitt Romney, Justin Trudeau, Caroline Mulroney, and now Oprah.

Winfrey first flirted with politics back in 2008 when she endorsed then–presidential candidate Barack Obama. It is estimated that her support of Obama generated more than a million votes for the candidate and played a significant role in his fundraising capacity.

Since then, Winfrey has never indicated she would be interested in running for the US presidency. As recently as this summer, Winfrey said, she would not run for public office, let alone for president.

How the tides have turned. And now, anticipation is running high. Oprah's speech at the Golden Globes on Sunday electrified audiences the world over and inspired media to spill thousands of barrels of ink on her potential presidential ambitions.

It triggered 3.1 billion social media impressions, the hashtag #Oprah2020 was part of 50,255 tweets, and the numbers go on.

Speculation about celebrities with political aspirations is not new. Just about every presidential election cycle since the Reagan years has seen celebrities hint about running.

However, those flirtations were usually dismissed as improbable, if not outright impossible. Conventional wisdom held that despite initial enthusiasm, the lack of conventional political infrastructure doomed these ventures from the start.

Trump's election to the presidency fundamentally altered that long-entrenched view.

The fact that news networks, pundits, social media, and water-cooler analysts are taking the #Oprah2020 hashtag seriously is because Trump has legitimized the idea that a celebrity can come from outside one of the two old-line political parties and take the Oval Office. As a result, a famous television host becoming the leader of the free world no longer seems crazy.

Perhaps more importantly, the speed and intensity with which Winfrey was able to gain legitimate momentum last week demonstrates that voters are willing to think seriously and differently about what type of person they want to hold high public office.

Does someone's celebrity alone qualify them to be president or prime minister? Does it matter what has made them famous?

Is this a new way of looking at things or is it merely an evolution of a path we have been on for some time?

It goes without saying, Oprah is in a class with very few others. She is a woman with a very significant following, and with good reason. She has acted as a spiritual leader and a symbol of unity in America for decades. She is one of only a handful of people who is recognizable on a first name–only basis.

There are persuasive arguments that a President Winfrey could be a healing presidency; one that may be sorely needed after four years of division under an aggressive president who has significantly exacerbated previously existing tensions.

But there remain other challenges.

The presidency of the United States, like all elected positions, doesn't come with training wheels. They are complex positions that require leadership, expertise, and experience; a sophisticated grasp of the intricacies of public policy; and a strong understanding of how power is wielded.

When it comes time to choose our leaders, hopefully we think about his or her experience, qualifications, love of country, dedication, purpose, ideology, and expertise in policy and legislative matters.

Hopefully, we don't think too much about a candidate's social media followers, television ratings, product lines, award acceptance speeches, hair, or whether they'd be a great person with whom to have a drink.

Celebrities often bring strong advocacy skills. They are often powerful at raising money, awareness, and changing people's opinions. They are often persuasive, empathetic, and expert communicators.

And that's a great start. But what doesn't follow is a fluency in the sphere of democratic institutions and public-policy initiatives. Being a democratic leader requires much more than speaking louder than everyone else. Or having more followers on Twitter.

The fix to what currently ails the American presidency is not more of what injured it in the first place. The challenges of this presidency, the challenges that so many Americans chafe against, will not be solved by doubling down. It may well be better to change course altogether.

MISSED THE BIG PICTURE

What was I thinking? Was I auditioning for a role as Pollyanna?

It seems that while I was rehearsing my lines, I missed a point fundamental to the discussion: our changing media landscape.

The celebrity-turned-politician is nothing new. An early incarnation of this trend is the war hero, like JFK. Then there was Reagan, the actor-turned-president. More recently, we've seen the likes of Dr. Oz and Caitlyn Jenner enter the fray and, mercifully, fail.

So, what *is* new, and why will we see more? Two answers.

First, social media has altered what is considered personal. While politics—in many corners of polite society—is still considered "personal," social media has blown open the doors of privacy. It's commonplace now for people to livestream from the bathroom and share intimate pictures as though they were Tic Tacs. It's hardly a surprise celebrities are now more willing, even wanting, to share their political views, because, well, they're sharing *everything else*.

Second, media coverage—the oxygen of celebrity life—has now conflated politics and entertainment. Entertainment has become political, and politics, entertainment. The fascinating trajectory of Ukrainian president Volodymyr Zelensky reflects this development. Here's a man who literally pretended to be president for a TV show before *reality* came calling. One might've expected this would be a recipe for disaster. And yet, the exact opposite has unfolded. Far from an entertainer or showman, Zelensky has proven to be a principled, serious leader capable of rallying his country to confront a grievous challenge. It turns out Mark Twain was correct: truth really is stranger than fiction.[13]

The trend of entertainers taking up politics will only continue. While this may imbue the vocation with a heightened sense of entertainment for the public, the stakes have not changed. The quality of our lives depends upon having effective, informed individuals in office. Their professional origins are moot.

But we must ensure a political career is no mere costume change. It's precisely *because* of these figures' pre-existing popularity and ability to perform that we must scrutinize their competence. Otherwise, we risk our politics becoming a badly scripted sitcom.

*The Ottawa Centre MP for the NDP set a sterling example of passion
and principle who strived to work with politicians from all parties.*

Don't Forget MP
Paul Dewar's Message
of Inclusiveness

With Paul Dewar's way-too-soon death, on Wednesday evening, Canadians lost a giant. A gentle, principled, passionate giant. A giant who dedicated his very life to the service of others.

There will be no shortage of epithets for Paul, but he would likely choose to be remembered for his honest and authentic engagement with his constituents, and for his commitment to their priorities—a commitment that never once wavered.

He will also be remembered as that rarest of parliamentarians: one who, while holding firm to his beliefs and loyalty to his party, set an example of civility and multi-partisan co-operation.

Many a Sunday, for example, I would hear from him about this column.

Dewar's political career was forged in the long shadow of his mother, Marion Dewar, who served as mayor of Ottawa from 1978 to 1985. Marion led Project 4000, which saw the establishment across Canada of over seven thousand private sponsorship groups for refugees of the Vietnam War. Her initiative influenced the federal government to increase Canada's refugee acceptance quota from eight thousand to sixty thousand.

Paul often spoke of how his mother shaped his view of politics, so it is unsurprising that Dewar's career was marked by a commitment to social activism and a belief in the potential of politics as a force for good.

After graduating from Queen's University, Paul taught Ottawa students with special needs, and then worked as an organizer for the Ottawa-Carleton Elementary Teachers' Federation.

In 2006, he ran as the NDP candidate for Ottawa Centre, and was elected to the House of Commons. His colleagues always commented on Dewar's commitment to his constituency, noting that he would attend community meetings even when they did not directly pertain to his responsibilities.

He had a collegial working relationship with his provincial counterpart, Liberal MPP Yasir Naqvi, another instance of his pragmatism taking precedence over party affiliation.

In his role as foreign affairs critic, Dewar was a loud voice for social justice around the world, and a champion for human rights. He pushed the Harper government to denounce nations with homophobic agendas, as in the cases of Russia's anti-LGBTQ2S+ legislation, and Uganda's 2014 Anti-Homosexuality Act.

Dewar also criticized the downsizing of Canada's role as peacekeeper, which he saw as crucial to our country's engagement with the international community.

At the time of his appointment as critic, foreign affairs discourse in the House was dominated by John Baird and Bob Rae. It is a testament to Dewar's graciousness and decency as a politician that he established strong working relationships with both men.

It is not often that a friendship of this kind develops between a minister and a critic. And yet, Minister Baird made a point of inviting Dewar to travel with him to the Middle East. The two also worked together on issues facing their neighbouring Ottawa ridings.

When Paul found out, in 2018, that his cancer was terminal, he did not retreat into his own problems. Instead, he devoted himself to Youth Action Now, an initiative that supports and provides funding for youth-led initiatives. Thanks to his work, a new generation will be introduced to the principles that drew him to public service.

In November, Dewar accepted the *Maclean's* Parliamentarian of the Year lifetime achievement award, and in his acceptance speech he struck a tone of collaboration. Speaking to the assembled politicians and journalists, he asked the crowd to remember the moment that first drew them to political work. He then asked them to turn to their neighbours and spend two minutes sharing their initial aspirations and ideas of what can be accomplished through public service.

"Is it not time," he asked, "to take off the armour of our political party and work together as people representing citizens to build a better country for everyone?"

Paul's message has never been truer than it is today. As we reflected when George H. W. Bush died earlier this year, there is no limit to what we can accomplish when we put differences aside and work together.

We could offer Paul no better final mitzvah, as our Jewish friends would say, than to heed this lesson as we go into the next election.

Dewar's "armour" metaphor is apt. It suggests we need protection to wage battle in the blood sport of politics. It also invokes garments worn as a sign of tribal identity. Identity provides meaning because it feels good to stand alongside others wearing the same uniform, fighting the same fight. And yet, large-scale challenges that might have unified Canadians in previous generations (like health crises and foreign interference) are currently refracted through a partisan lens—and our society suffers for it.

So, I wish I had offered a few words from the man himself.

> In my time on this earth, I was passionate about the power of citizens working together and making a difference.
>
> I wanted a Canada where we treat our fellow citizens with the dignity, love, and respect that every one of us deserves.

I wanted a world where we reduced suffering and increased happiness. A world where we took better care of each other.

I had the privilege to travel and see that despite our many unique differences, we are all ultimately driven by the same desires for community, belonging, and fairness.

It is easy sometimes to feel overwhelmed by the gravity of the challenges we face. Issues like climate change, forced migration, and the threat posed by nuclear weapons. It's hard to know how to make a difference.

The secret is not to focus on how to solve the problem but concentrate on what you can contribute—to your country, your community, and neighbours.

Start from a place of compassion and be grateful for all that Canada has to offer . . .[14]

It takes a courageous person to step into "no man's land" the way Dewar called us to do, away from the intellectual comfort of our entrenched beliefs. He challenged his political peers and fellow citizens to climb out of their foxholes of certainty and superiority. In the heat of political conflict, this can seem impossible. But through his life's work, Paul encouraged us to see our world differently.

In death, in his final public statement, he did the same. Let's do our best to honour his challenge.

Besides astonishing political theatre, Jody Wilson-Raybould's testimony also sounding a warning to Canadians that the burden she faced as being both the attorney general and the minister of justice stemmed, at least in part, from a structural flaw in our political system.

Wilson-Raybould Testimony Nothing If Not a Roman Spectacle

On Wednesday afternoon, in an event that exceeded its considerable billing, Canada's former attorney general and minister of justice, Jody Wilson-Raybould, filled in many of the contours of Bob Fife's early-February reporting that thrust the prime minister, his closest advisers, and the Liberal Party of Canada into a political firestorm.

Her testimony was as astonishing as it was remarkable in its candour, and willingness to draw blood.

Wilson-Raybould named names and read records: phone calls, emails, text messages, and contemporaneous meeting notes. She told a story of a coordinated and persistent effort by the machinery of government—PMO and PCO alike—to influence her decision-making.

She vividly recalled veiled threats and potential personal consequences. Her recollection of ten phone calls and ten meetings contradicted Michael Wernick, the clerk of the privy council.

Her language conveyed, in a straightforward way, her conviction that an injustice had taken place.

And, yet when the dust settled, there remained so much more to be said.

What has the PMO not allowed the former AG to say? Why was she not released to discuss her time as minister of veteran affairs and her resignation from cabinet?

And then beyond the former minister herself, what will others have to say? How will Gerry Butts use his appearance before the Standing Committee on Justice and Human Rights to recast the government's narrative?

What about all the other people Wilson-Raybould named?

And above all, how will *l'affaire* SNC-Lavalin play out in Quebec versus the rest of Canada? Which parties' electoral fortunes will it help? Whose will it hurt?

While we wait for answers to these, and many more questions, specific to this matter, we'd do well to think about some of the things which gave rise to this mess at first instance.

Lisa Raitt, deputy leader of the opposition, asked Wilson-Raybould on Wednesday if this experience had left her with anything she thinks should be recommended to Parliament.

Wilson-Raybould's response was instructive.

"I've thought about this a lot," she said, "and I think this committee [should] look at the role of the minister of justice and the attorney general of Canada, and whether or not those two roles should be bifurcated."

She went on to say that there should be consideration around "having the AG not sit around the cabinet table."

In hindsight, it's plainly clear she has a point.

While there are procedural and practical arguments for dividing the roles, perhaps the most important argument for doing so is the simple fact it is unreasonable to ask one person to perform two contradictory roles.

Is it not, on its face, absurd to think that one person can, one minute, be expected to act in a non-partisan way and then in literally the next minute to act as a partisan?

In our system, the minister of justice is inherently partisan: she or he is responsible for drafting partisan policy and shepherding partisan legislation through Parliament on behalf of the governing party.

The attorney general, on the other hand, is the chief law officer of the Crown, responsible for the government's litigation and for providing legal advice regarding the very policies they have—while wearing their minister of justice "hat"—helped to draft.

In the United Kingdom, the role of the secretary of state for justice, who has oversight of the ministry of justice, is separate and distinct from the attorney general, who is the chief legal adviser to the Crown and oversees prosecutions but is not usually a member of cabinet.

And when the AG has sat in cabinet, problems have arisen. Prime Minister Blair's AG Lord Goldsmith came to a "better view" of the legality of the Iraq War ten days after conversations with the prime minister and his cabinet. And the rest, as they say, is history.

When Jody Wilson-Raybould speaks of the strain that she has been subject to, she refers, of course, to "political interference." But she is also sounding a warning to Canadians that the burden she faced stemmed, at least in part, from a structural flaw in our political system.

CUT TO THE CHASE

Our political systems rely on balance in order to function properly. When the three sections of government—the legislative, executive, and judicial branches—are functioning as they were intended to, the people of democratic countries can expect a government that is reliable, efficient, and accountable. It's a delicate balance.

The danger is when one branch becomes more powerful or influential than it's supposed to be. If that happens, the whole enterprise quickly falls apart.

Ms. Wilson-Raybould describes in the above column the serious hazards of partisanship bleeding into what is supposed to be a system of non-partisan justice. Take, for instance, the rise of authoritarian leaders in many (previously) democratic countries. By incrementally increasing their power over other branches of government (particularly the judicial branch) these leaders undermine the checks and balances built into democratic systems. These are extreme examples, no doubt, but they are well worth paying attention to.

While all justice systems carry the biases of their creators, many functional ones have attempted to rise above these biases by analyzing judicial issues through a contemporary lens, incorporating aspects of restorative justice into traditionally retributive systems. But partisan influence, especially from the executive branch, can seriously jeopardize the integrity of our judicial systems. The "War on Drugs" is one such example.

Situations like those Wilson-Raybould found herself in are minor when compared to those in the United States, where judges often express support for the politicians who appointed them rather than show the impartiality one would hope they would use to decide the case before them. It's worse in countries with higher rates of political corruption, such as Venezuela, where entire elections can be stolen.

So, Ms. Wilson-Raybould was correct: she was at a conflict of interest. I was right to examine this weakness. We can never excuse such events as isolated incidents. It doesn't matter how challenging the task might be or where it takes us, we simply have to remove every last bit of partisanship we possibly can from the judicial process. Remove the attorney general from the cabinet. *Point finale.*

May 5, 2019

*The lieutenant-governor has used her bully pulpit to help provide everyday
citizens with answers to their important questions and has done so in a
way that models an approach that partisan politicians
would do well to emulate.*

Lieutenant-Governor Dowdeswell Using Her Bully Pulpit to Better Society

I n the cut and thrust of the increasingly divisive and polarizing way politics are being practised today, one of the most worrisome developments is the loss of the bully pulpit.

In some ways an old-fashioned notion, today's practitioners seem to have forgotten its power of moral suasion to forge consensus and to truly lead.

The notion of the bully pulpit came to prominence in the administration of Theodore Roosevelt, who realized the presidency afforded him an unparalleled platform to promote his priorities and outlook for the nation. Roosevelt took advantage of the prestige of the White House and cultivated relationships in order to convince Americans—and in turn, an intransigent Congress—that the challenges of industrialization required drastic measures in the form of regulation.

Today, politicians have come, wrongly in my point of view, to believe that the bully pulpit itself is no longer a powerful tool. Rather, they favour announcements, programs, and spending.

As one premier once told me, "I don't get out of bed to announce anything less than one hundred million dollars."

The result? Public discourse has become transactional rather than aspirational. More and more, it has become focused on the *here and now* at the expense of building a better tomorrow.

One civil society leader, instructively not a politician, who understands the power of the bully pulpit—in spades—is Ontario's lieutenant-governor, the Honourable Elizabeth Dowdeswell.

Her Honour deeply understands this platform and its uses. In fact, she refers to herself as the province's "storyteller-in-chief," and broke with tradition in her inaugural speech by stressing not her priority focus but instead her commitment to use the office as a forum for reflection and "a crucible for ideas."

On Tuesday evening, I watched Dowdeswell in action in her suite at Queen's Park as she delivered a speech to open her latest exhibit, *Speaking of Democracy*, and provided a textbook example of the bully pulpit in practice.

Her Honour spoke of the strictly non-partisan nature of her role, and her duty as the guarantor of responsible governance. She noted that viceregal representatives have been described "as a conscience . . . representing the hearts, minds, and souls of citizens."

She then went on to make a point that has stuck with me.

"Democracy," she said, "is about so much more than government. It is about . . . how we learn to live together on this planet in peace and harmony. And so, I ask questions, hoping to evoke the best of ourselves."

While Dowdeswell has clearly mastered the use of the bully pulpit, she also benefits from our Canadian system of government with its viceregal offices spread across the country.

As representatives of the Crown in Canada, governors general and lieutenant-governors alike have an opportunity to reach Canadians in a truly unique way. Well beyond their purely ceremonial duties and important institutional role, viceroys can focus their tenure in office on specific initiatives that appeal to our better angels: for Michaëlle Jean it was freedom and cultural integration, for David Johnston, philanthropy and volunteering, for Dowdeswell, issues of citizenship, democracy, the environment and Indigenous reconciliation.

What's more, they can make their offices truly inclusive and accessible.

Since being invested in 2014, Her Honour has commissioned five exhibitions, accepted over fifty thousand visitors to her suite in Queen's Park and conducted more than 3,300 engagements. She has represented Ontario on international visits from Utah to the UK, France, Italy, and Switzerland, making the case for Ontario's place in the world. Most importantly, she has visited over 110 ridings across the province, promoting citizenship and meeting with Ontarians to hear their perspectives on the well-being of community and civil society.

In doing so, the lieutenant-governor has used her bully pulpit to help provide everyday citizens with answers to their important questions and has done so in a way that models an approach that partisan politicians would do well to emulate.

A more skilful and effective use of the pulpit is hard to imagine.

I find it fascinating that the whole construct of viceregal representatives, an undemocratic vestige from our colonial past, can be used to promote democracy in meaningful ways.

The finest quote from Dowdeswell's *Speaking of Democracy* exhibition comes from the French writer Édouard Louis. It goes:

> Among those who have everything, politics changes almost nothing. What's strange is that they're the ones who engage in politics. Though it has almost no effect on their lives. For the ruling class, in general, politics is a question of aesthetics: a way of seeing themselves, of seeing the world, of constructing a personality. For us it was life or death.[15]

The dominant aspect of Dowdeswell's efforts to promote democracy is that, although her role of lieutenant-governor comes with trappings, pomp, and ceremony, for her it's not about the "ruling class"—it's about everybody else.

For so many, our politics appears to be a maze of callous politicos and egotistical maniacs. In sum, everyday citizens decide that politics is not *for them* and, as a result, disengage. When citizens feel the political process does not and cannot reflect their beliefs, the road to significant political unrest is never far.

Dowdeswell's genius has been to bring democracy back into people's lives by explaining that it's about "about how we choose to live together."[16]

So, I ask: What is a viceregal office but the person who holds it? While you could argue this is true for every public-office holder, the stakes are different for viceregals. They can't be voted out of office. They're not called to defend their views in Question Period each day. And so, the choice is theirs. They can sit on their hands all day and do nothing, or they can do some good.

Since I wrote this column, the remarkable number of impactful engagements Elizabeth Dowdeswell has carried out in every corner of Ontario has only grown. So too has the tremendous impact she's made on civic life.

Time for a prediction. Elizabeth Dowdeswell, the doyenne of democracy, will go down as one of the most effective and well-liked lieutenant-governors in Canadian history.

May 31, 2020

Canada's ambassador to China was a savvy choice. An experienced China hand, and a principled realist, he now uses the qualities that enabled him to succeed brilliantly in business to drive his candid commentary about China.

Dominic Barton Is Canada's Bright Light in the Crisis with China

When it comes to China, the Trudeau government has acted with the deference a pageboy would show a queen. As they have muddled through a long series of skirmishes, from the arbitrary and unjust kidnapping of Michael Kovrig and Michael Spavor to the trade disputes over canola, soybeans, and meat, the objections of the federal government have been muted and overly diplomatic.

For a time, it seemed the COVID-19 pandemic would be no different. The well-substantiated suggestion that China had been less than forthcoming in its disclosures about the virus was dismissed by the federal health minister as a "conspiracy theory." The minister of foreign affairs twisted himself into a pretzel to avoid even saying the word "Taiwan." We refused to close our border to flights originating from China. And this week, as Beijing snuffed out the last remnants of the "one country, two systems" agreement that protected civil liberties in Hong Kong, the most Trudeau could muster was a call for "constructive" dialogue.

But thankfully, a bright light has appeared on the horizon: plucked from the private sector and appointed Canadian ambassador to China last September, Dominic Barton has gone further than any other Canadian official in criticizing Beijing.

Last week, Barton was in the news for his comments to the Canadian International Council in which he suggested Beijing had accrued "negative soft power" through its belligerent international response to the COVID-19 pandemic, and endorsed a "rigorous review" of the World Health Organization's response.

By the standard of the Trudeau government, this amounted to surprisingly pointed criticism. More surprising still was the prime minister's endorsement of this criticism the day after it was reported publicly.

Some had early concerns with Barton, who was appointed to the ambassadorship fresh off his stint as the managing director of the consulting firm McKinsey.

But Barton was a savvy choice. An experienced China hand, and a principled realist, he now uses the qualities that enabled him to succeed brilliantly in business to drive his candid commentary about China.

It is helpful that his concerns are real. In bungling its so-called mask diplomacy, China has, indeed, eroded its soft power and further alienated foreign governments. The Netherlands was forced to recall six hundred thousand faulty masks bought from China; in Spain, fifty thousand test kits were tossed out after it was discovered they were only accurate about one-in-three times. The Slovenians bought 1.2 million antibody tests for sixteen million dollars, only to discover they were similarly useless. The Czechs have had complaints, and so have the Turks. And, of course, Canada too. The list goes on.

Through it all, the Chinese government has pushed aggressively, in a Trump-like way, for the leaders of these European nations to offer public displays of gratitude. But the gambit has backfired. Instead of gratitude, the EU's chief diplomat has warned that this so-called politics of generosity disguises a "geopolitical struggle for influence through spinning."

And so it is these two ambassadors who, in positions not known for straight talk, have emerged as the sanest, clearest moral voice when it comes to China.

Of course, there will always be a David-and-Goliath dynamic that constrains what Canadians can say and do when it comes to dealing with a superpower such as China. The reality is Ottawa cannot simultaneously be at odds with both Beijing and Washington, especially while the latter has its mercurial commander-in-chief.

Nevertheless, I predict we can count on Barton to continue to speak truth to power, at least so much as his position—and Canada's position—allows.

And speak truth to power not just to the Chinese but to the Canadian government as well. After all, he has the tools to do so: credibility and respect within Trudeau's Ottawa and within Xi's Beijing.

But doing so just got more complicated. On Wednesday, a BC judge decided the case against Meng Wanzhou, a Huawei executive and daughter of the company's founder, should proceed.

Though the courts have yet to rule on her extradition to the US, the ultimate decision-maker in this process is the minister of justice, who must determine whether the extradition could generate an outcome that runs "contrary to Canadian values."

Contrary to Canadian values when it comes to China? Watch for Barton's influence as the Trudeau government works to sort that question.

COULDN'T SEE
IT COMING

First things first. The Michaels are home and that is something that every Canadian, regardless of political stripe, should celebrate.

Their release signals, as well, that I was correct: Barton was the right individual for this task. A job that—let's face it—*he didn't have to take*. A role that required extraordinary commitment and service. A job that all could see would be a mountainous challenge.

These factors being what they were, you would expect (and this point is implicit in my column) that *if* Barton *did* conquer that summit and help release the two Michaels from their horrific squalor and maltreatment, he would have secured himself a hero's welcome here in Canada and enjoyed near-universal praise.

Unfortunately, in the years since Barton resigned as ambassador to China in December 2021, virtually the exact opposite has unfolded due to a 2023 scandal involving the extent of McKinsey's contracts with the federal government. For the Conservatives, Barton became a convenient symbol of Liberal insiderism.[17] They attacked his character and accomplishments over many media cycles. Hardly the thank-you medal he deserved.

This column failed to anticipate that the Michaels' release would not signal some magical détente. That Canada's relationship with China would only sour was predictable. How Barton's noble service would be spun for political points wasn't.

And therein lies an important lesson in the domain of leadership. No matter how hard you try, context will always be more powerful than you.

Furthermore, there was never a more powerful example of "what makes you rich, makes you poor." Everything that made, as I say, Barton a "savvy choice" for Trudeau and successful in his post was used to lambaste him. Critics spun his credentials as "an experienced China hand" and internationally successful businessman into a selfish globalist with no love for dear ol' Canada.

Yet, Barton can be content knowing that he is, quintessentially, that "individual in the arena" Roosevelt spoke of, who can assure himself that it's "not the critic who counts," but rather the individual who "spends himself in a worthy cause."[18]

January 10, 2022

The stain of Andrew's alleged behaviour is something different from past royal scandals—the litany of affairs, divorces, and other human failings.

Prince Andrew's Legal Manoeuvring Over Sexual-Abuse Suit Jeopardizes the Foundation of the Monarchy

The House of Windsor is no stranger to a good scandal: The abdication crisis. Charles and Camilla. "Megxit."

But far from an episode of *The Crown*, which contains the fallout within a neat fifty-eight minutes, all of these crises have had long-term repercussions for the institution of the monarchy. Specifically, they have undermined its image as being the paragon of those quintessential British values: probity, having thick skin, and above all, steadiness.

Yet, for all these issues, Queen Elizabeth II still reigns, Buckingham Palace still stands, and the Commonwealth remains an important political force in the world. Indeed, the British monarchy is matched only by the Vatican as a centuries-old institution that has maintained its stature in a rapidly changing world.

That was, of course, until Prince Andrew.

New revelations emerged this week about the Duke of York's efforts to stymie a sexual-abuse suit launched by one of Jeffrey Epstein's accusers. For years, the Royal Family has been rocked by Andrew's long-time association with the convicted sex offender. And for years, Andrew has done the bare minimum to deny any wrongdoing.

But now, as his legal team pushes back hard against accuser Virginia Giuffre, the charade seems to be ending.[19]

Having botched his primary attempt to publicly refute the claims—an interview with BBC heavyweight Emily Maitlis—Andrew has instead tried to weasel his way out of the conversation altogether.[20]

First, he tried to avoid being served with legal papers.

Failing that, his team now contends that Andrew is immune from the civil suit under the restrictions of a previous Epstein settlement.

To make their point, they have claimed that Andrew qualifies as a "potential defendant" in Giuffre's earlier case against Epstein. For all the legal complexity of the assertion, it seems to put the lie to Andrew's claim of never having met Giuffre.

No one who has seen Andrew's BBC interview[21] will be surprised. As time goes on, his excuses grow more brazen, contrived, and bizarre. What's more, the tactics of his legal team represent a new low for the monarchy in their depravity and detachment from reality.

And therein lies the real problem.

In the past, when scandals have thrown the royals' unsavoury private lives into public view, the moral and religious authority of their brand has been eroded. But the stain of Andrew's accusations is something different. Unlike the litany of affairs, divorces, and other human failings, his alleged behaviour appears criminal—and his response, simply unacceptable.

Rather than clear his name, the duke seems content to feign indignation at the idea that he should be accountable to anyone. In doing so, he has left his family with little alternative but to remain silent about the allegations. The result makes them appear entirely out of touch at a time when they urgently need to appear modern and suited for the moment.

For example, Andrew retains his military titles and remains a member of the Royal Family—albeit one removed from public life. This seems bizarre given that his nephew, Prince Harry, was stripped of his own military titles for abdicating his royal duties and leaving Britain.

It stinks of hypocrisy.

All this takes place amidst a major shift for the House of Windsor. Nearly seventy years into her reign, many are certain it will be impossible for the Queen's successor to enjoy the same popularity and presence on the world stage. After all, the British royals are the exception, not the norm, among a litany of European monarchies whose faces are entirely unknown outside their own borders.

If Prince Andrew settles his case with Giuffre—likely to the tune of millions of pounds—he and his family could ultimately pay a much greater price. Not only does the duke run the risk of being confirmed as a sex offender, but he could also potentially be confirmed a liar. And what's even worse, one whose own family abetted his lies.

BACK TO THE DRAWING BOARD

The headline-grabbing scandals surrounding Prince Andrew and Prince Harry are not the first to threaten the House of Windsor, nor will they be the last.

Indeed, for those who think the monarchy is a waste of time and money, anachronistic and meaningless, these views were only reinforced. For other Canadians, the actions of these subsidiary royals did not impact their feelings on the monarchy because their views were attached to the Queen herself and not to the institution. The Queen always seemed to be above everything, separate. A constant institution that all her subjects could trust. Her death destroyed that institution, and the one that came to replace it looks far closer to the ground.

And it's for this reason that the death of the Queen and the accession of Charles to the throne poses the biggest challenge for the Crown in Canada.

While obviously not helpful, I don't think the bad behaviour of a couple of princes ultimately matters much to Canadians who don't hold strong views of the monarchy. It's all just part of an oversaturated entertainment cycle. What does matter is that Charles has been unable to forge a meaningful bond with Canadians. So the fact that Charles is not his mother—and never can be—that is the monarchy's real existential problem. It is simply impossible for Charles, though he has tried, to establish a connection with Canada that is as strong as the one his mother forged. A problem that, for the Crown, may well be insurmountable.

Whatever happens, wherever we end up (and I'm not taking bets yet), it won't come about because of a frozen penis or other lurid revelations (sorry, Harry).[22] It will come about because of the serious disconnect between the Crown and Canada.

January 23, 2022

Johnson appears to be betting on either the desperation, alienation, or stupidity of the British electorate. I am not sure which is most offensive.

Boris Johnson's Latest Circus Is More than a Failure of Morals—It's Poor Crisis Management

After a long period at the top of the polls, British prime minister Boris Johnson is staring down the barrel.

Furor is intensifying around revelations that he and his staff not just broke, but repeatedly flouted, his own government's COVID restrictions—the very restrictions he imposed on the rest of the country.[23] Now the opposition, the public, and indeed Johnson's own backbenchers are out for blood.

But perhaps most contemptible of all have been the prime minister's own attempts to save his skin, clawing at any opportunity he has to abdicate his responsibilities.

There is no strategy here. I can only surmise that Johnson and his advisers are betting on either the desperation, alienation, or stupidity of their electorate. I am not sure which is most offensive to the British people. Take your pick.

To recap for those not following this saga: the PM was caught red-handed attending several parties that occurred, of all places, at his official residence, 10 Downing Street—in direct contravention of his government's own stringent restrictions at the peak of lockdown. At a time when most Britons couldn't leave their house except for essentials, Boris permitted drinks and mingling in his own back garden.

Most humiliatingly, he was obliged to publicly apologize to the Queen for a party that took place on the eve of the late Prince Philip's funeral—a funeral at which Her Majesty chose to very publicly observe the lockdown measures and sit alone.[24]

Shameful doesn't even begin to describe it.

First, Johnson claimed that he was not aware the "bring your own booze" events (astonishingly, that was actually included in the invitations) were social occasions. He then said the parties were coordinated by his rambunctious staff without his knowledge or blessing. More ludicrously, he later suggested that he was not informed of the rules banning such gatherings—despite having signed off on them himself![25]

The entire pathetic ordeal has led me to the grim conclusion that in Britain, as in many corners of the world, a period of sustained disruption and reliance on government has endowed elected leaders with an air of hubris. But as Johnson is learning, it is a mistake to equate a "rallying around the flag" response with a free pass to behave as you like.

One of the fundamental tenets of crisis response is that there is no substitute for leading with compassion. Johnson's actions not only represent an appalling indifference to his responsibilities as prime minister—they are also a total abdication of leadership.

By blaming the culture within his office, Johnson has opted for the lowest excuse possible. And now, his plan is to use an external investigation to throw his team under the bus, in another abandonment of his leadership duties.

As a rule of thumb, if you need an investigation to assess your own conduct, your problem is almost always one of principles.

A true leader, or at least what we used to consider a leader, would have fallen on their sword and accepted responsibility for the rotten culture oozing from Number 10. And ironically, in doing so, they may have saved their own hide.

But not Boris Johnson. In a cheap ploy to win back hearts and minds of the Tory backbench as much as the British public, he even went so far as to lift virtually all pandemic restrictions. [26]

But our British cousins are not alone. We've seen our own political leaders behave badly as well.

Time and again, we allow our politicians to mask their abject failures through the new-found, outsized role they play in our lives. Hiding behind the ups and downs of a pandemic, they behave as though adversity has made people completely passive.

It is high time to prove them wrong, by reminding ourselves that behaviour in public life matters—particularly when so much has been asked of our country.

NAILED IT

Boris Johnson ultimately resigned later that year in July 2022. This scandal (which became known as "partygate") proved to be a leading factor in his undoing.

Johnson's lone solace these days might be that at least he fared better than his successor, Liz Truss, the shortest-serving PM in the UK's history, who stepped down principally due to a failed tax-cutting budget that rocked financial markets. While comparisons of Boris's appearance to an ungroomed poodle or alpaca were always unkind, the comparison of Truss (more specifically her tenure) to a slowly rotting lettuce was both hilarious and far crueller.[27]

Johnson was never able to fall on his sword. Only after having been fined for contravening lockdown rules did he finally manage an apology to the British people in the Commons—albeit one that Labour leader Sir Keir Starmer neatly summarized as a "joke," commenting, "Even now, as the latest mealy-mouthed apology stumbles out of one side of [his] mouth, a new set of deflections and distortions pours from the other."[28] Devastating.

This utter failure to offer his full contrition, even once all the facts had come to light, only proves my point that it was Johnson's profound arrogance—his inability to understand that the rules that apply to everyone else also apply to him—that secured his downfall.

I would add just one thing. Johnson famously studied classics at Balliol College, Oxford, after—why, of course—Eton. One of my favourite Greek myths is that of Bellerophon, the hero who tamed the winged horse, Pegasus. One day, yearning to peer into the heavens, he urged Pegasus to fly high enough to see Olympus. The gods didn't exactly like that; they sent Bellerophon hurtling back to earth—to spend the rest of his days wandering in search of his beloved horse.

Johnson's Pegasus was his popularity with the British people, and his heights had an address: 10 Downing Street. Now, like Bellerophon without his steed, Johnson without his office is a nobody, a former PM crashing about looking for anything, just anything, to do.

February 27, 2022

Biden must remind Americans why engagement is not an option. He must offer a "Biden doctrine," rooted in the hard lessons of certain conflicts.

Joe Biden Is Correct to Keep Soldiers Out of Ukraine—Now He Must Explain Why, And What Comes Next

Any discussion of Russia-Ukraine should begin with an acknowledgement that millions will be devastated by Vladimir Putin's illegal invasion. Lives will be lost and a great price will be paid in terms of Ukraine's political viability and long-term prospects.

It is heartbreaking to watch a country that has made such profound and hard-won progress fall prey to the whims of an autocrat. Yet, it is our duty to watch. To bear witness. To remember.

Indeed, it is the tragedy of our modern world that technology has given us unprecedented windows into human suffering around the globe, while our political reality has made it harder to *do* much about it.

Western governments are trying. The sanctions announced this week will devastate Russia's economy. What's to come will be even worse. And yet, it's hard to escape the feeling that our response does not amount to much.

Western citizens are now used to watching helplessly as despots trample the international order. While the reality on the ground could not be more different, the surreal emotions of this week echoed those of August, as we watched the Taliban enter Kabul.

For good reason, political leaders have decided that the alternative is far worse. Direct military engagement with a nuclear power is off the table—particularly one as volatile and brazen as Russia. And even if the US were prepared to respond with force, European allies would not condone it. Inaction is, nonetheless, a bitter pill to swallow.

The Western role, then, is by and large a moral one. NATO allies will condemn Putin at every turn and assert their support for Ukraine. The UN Security Council will consider motions to chasten Putin, but they are unlikely to pass. Adding salt to the wound, Russian ambassador Vasily Nebenzya is presently serving as president of the council—an egregious conflict of interest in any other setting.[29]

The failings of multilateral organizations to prevent this egregious violation of international law will not easily be forgotten, and we can expect to emerge from this a more divided world.

Centre stage in all this is US president Joe Biden, a man determined to avoid the mistakes of his predecessors. His measured approach is informed by both history and memory.

Various lawmakers have invoked the legacy of appeasement and British PM Neville Chamberlain's failure to stop Hitler in his tracks. The metaphor is powerful but self-serving. Perhaps instead of Czechoslovakia in 1938, Biden is thinking more of Afghanistan and Iraq—to say nothing of Bosnia, Vietnam, or other examples of American intervention gone awry.

Yet, Biden has not explicitly made the case against intervention, choosing instead to laud NATO and emphasize his sanctions. To the bafflement of many, the US will watch as Kyiv is trampled under the feet of a dictator.

In his first State of the Union Address this Tuesday, the president must remind Americans why engagement is not an option—and crucially, lay out his vision for a re-imagined world order. In short, he must offer a "Biden doctrine" rooted in the lessons of certain conflicts and tied to a faction of the intelligence community that is highly skeptical of American intervention.

As we've seen, this administration is keen to share the rationale and context behind their decision-making, even publishing classified intelligence with unprecedented zeal.

Now it's time for the president to do the same before a joint session of Congress, with the entire world watching. It will be the most crucial—and perhaps final—chance for Biden to spell out why the US has done relatively little in the face of so much suffering.

Biden must also set the stage for where the Western alliance is headed, beyond feel-good talk of co-operation. As Biden knows well, his decisions will have consequences for decades to come.

And for once, the American president is all too familiar with those immortal words: "What's past is prologue."

Now he must translate that message into method.

On February 24, 2022, the day Putin launched his illegal invasion of Ukraine, I had other things on my mind. I was waiting to begin the eight-hour operation that would give me a new kidney. As I drifted off to sleep in the operating room, I felt hopeful for a whole new life. A short while after I woke up, I realized that my new life had been placed in a new context.

Now, looking back, in far better health than I was, I can fully appreciate just how tense things were in the weeks leading up to the war.

Undoubtedly contributing to this tension was a bold strategy, exercised by the US State Department, to continually declassify and disclose intelligence on the Russian army's plans and movements. This strategy helped bring the major Western powers swiftly into alignment to isolate Russia economically soon after the invasion started.

Authenticity of information is, after all, crucial in times of war. For example, only hours after WWII commenced, Roosevelt took to the airwaves to declare that while the nation would remain neutral, Americans should not ignore the fact of Nazi aggression.

Of course, it takes sound information to make good decisions. But equally, people need to *believe* in that information's accuracy. In 1939, Roosevelt had only to assure the American people his information was genuine. In 2022, in a radically transformed information landscape, Biden had to reveal classified intel.

Both Roosevelt and Biden knew what they were doing: using information to sway public opinion. Roosevelt felt that the facts of Hitler's brutal invasion of sovereign territories would cause the American people to oppose him. And Biden obviously believed that by providing his citizens with the latest intelligence about a similarly unjust invasion, they would feel much the same way about Putin.

The echoes of history do not end here. Soon after Roosevelt's speech, the US supported the Allies by selling them arms on a cash-and-carry basis. In much the same way, after Russia's invasion of Ukraine, the American government supported Ukraine's defence through enormous donations of money and weapons.

3

In Power

The Perils of Governing

For members of the opposition, official or otherwise, holding the government to account is in the job description. And, with any luck, the best at it are elected to govern.

For political journalists, it's much the same. They view it as their obligation to sift through a politician's carefully curated rhetoric, glib replies, and non-answers to deliver a straighter truth. And while journalists hold themselves to be a part of the "fourth estate," which is to say *outside* the traditional domains of power, many are most certainly *not* outside our nation's political bubble. Put it this way: Ottawa's West Block, for example, is not a vast expanse. At its core, it is a small company town, where everyone knows everyone, where politicians and journalists (far from the mortal enemies they're often portrayed to be) get along just fine.

Columnists are, of course, right in the middle, perhaps even at the very centre, of this mix. We are not free from ideological or partisan leanings. And we don't (in most cases) purport to be. Rather, most of us are quite forthright in declaring that we have ideological or partisan leanings. Full disclosure, I am an old-fashioned Red Tory. Fiscally conservative. A believer in equality of opportunity, not outcome. A social progressive. A disciple of the Charter. A believer in the potential of the human spirit and, at my core, a very proud Canadian, but I digress.

And so, what we columnists do purport to offer, and *should* offer, is an entirely fresh perspective. While it's true that many of us emerge from within the political bubble, it's essential that we provide opinions from outside the consensus that often forms within it. And that's what I have always tried to bring to my columns: insight that arises from my experience.

I strive to bring that experience to bear, particularly when I am writing about the subtleties of governing. The simple truth is that it's very hard to truly understand government unless you've worked in or very close to it. Fortunately, I have. And I feel my perspective as a columnist is most valuable to my reader when offering my perspective about the impossible decisions governments must make—especially when they're acting upon incomplete information.

Governing is a field that requires demystification. Therefore, though I do not shrink from my label of "Conservative strategist," I do not believe it is the most revealing aspect of my resumé. More significant is the fact that I am privileged to have served and advised a range of government leaders. Apart from some of the especially partisan stands that I take from time to time, a "Liberal strategist," who also holds experience advising government leaders, might lend much of the same insight.

There is a saying by the English novelist John Galsworthy, "Idealism increases in direct proportion to one's distance from the problem."[30] Few things have been written so relevant to the nature of leadership and politics. In my experience, those working in government are both very close and very far away from certain problems. This relative distance shapes their view on what is possible and impossible. The same person acting as a misguided dreamer on one file might behave as an ice-cold pragmatist on another.

Yet, crucially, Galsworthy's statement applies with equal power to the expectations of the governed. Those not "in power" all share in a sort of common distance not only from the major problems governments confront but also from the problems of governing itself—the nuances, dynamics, and endless complexities.

And yet, our trust and belief in the government as an institution is framed by these expectations: which issues should be prioritized, which problems can and should be solved, in what manner, and how quickly.

I have tried to bring my readers a closer, more intimate view of these challenges in my columns on the politics and perils of governing, of being "in power."

The following columns cover a wide range of topics, from the nature of forgiveness to the rise of social media, from the politics of legalization to the complexion of majority rule. In each, I sought to apply my experience to some of those most polarizing and intriguing issues of the day. And after the retrospective exercise of writing this book, I have two overall observations that are intimately connected. First, I see many striking similarities and patterns in our politics and, on the whole, see an overriding sense of civility and good intentions. Second, in Canada, despite whatever might get said in the heat of political battle, we are tremendously lucky to have truly remarkable women and men who selflessly serve our nation for the greater good and who are deeply mindful of the fact that true power lies with the people and the people alone. For this, we should be deeply grateful. I know I am.

January 20, 2017

The Trudeau government has navigated the challenges well thus far,
but a Trump presidency fundamentally alters the waters.

Convulsing American Elephant Will Test Justin Trudeau's Agility

I t's perhaps ironic that it is an iconic quote by Prime Minister Justin Trudeau's father that sums up the situation that confronts him today. Pierre Trudeau once remarked that living next to the United States was "in some ways like sleeping with an elephant. No matter how friendly or even-tempered is the beast . . . one is affected by every twitch and grunt."

Trudeau's relationship with former president Barack Obama was often compared by the media to Brian Mulroney's infamously close relationship with Ronald Reagan; his relationship with Hillary Clinton, once cast as the inevitable successor to Obama, was no less warm.

Together, this promised a golden era of Liberal and Democratic rule in North America that would include increased environmental regulation, a focus on growing the social safety net, and, increasingly, aligned foreign policies that would emphasize brokering international peace rather than imposing it.

Friday's inauguration of Donald Trump as the forty-fifth president of the United States has suddenly, abruptly, rudely ruptured that idyllic vision.

The elephant isn't so much twitching as having full-body convulsions.

Following its election in 2015, the Liberal Party mapped out a four-year guide to re-election. They did this thinking they would have an American counterpart marching in lockstep on major policies.

Instead, the Liberals now face a president with plans antithetical to core components of their platform.

That said, the Trudeau government has shown it understands the enormity of the challenges it faces. The irascible Stéphane Dion has been shuffled out of the global affairs portfolio in favour of Chrystia Freeland who, in addition to having performed well at international trade, knows the United States well. A team specifically focused on US-Canada policy, led by Brian Clow, the very capable former chief of staff to Freeland has been drafted. High-level staff members have been dispatched to Trump Tower to meet with Trump administration officials.

And yet the enormity of the challenge has only begun to present itself, a challenge that will come in three principal forms.

The first is environmental policy. Carbon pricing grew increasingly popular with the Democratic establishment as the US election approached. It is very possible that increased environmental taxation would have been a top priority for Hillary Clinton. But that reality does not exist: President Trump is uncompromisingly opposed to any increase in business regulation for environmental purposes, a position at odds with the Trudeau government's decision to enact carbon pricing.

With a president who opposes environmental policies he sees as harming business and who favours reducing taxes, the Trudeau government could be forced to reconsider its commitment to a policy that will handicap Canadian businesses. Already, there has been pressure from our business community wary of the challenge.

The second challenge surrounds foreign policy. Again, the Trudeau government had found itself largely aligned with the less aggressive positioning of the Democratic establishment. A reluctance to be drawn into commitments on regional conflicts, support for increased consensus-building, and support of international institutions defined both the Obama and Trudeau administrations.

As Trump moves into the Oval Office, that harmony moves out. Even during the few short months following the election, he has demonstrated a belligerent, anti-establishment approach. NAFTA, the European Union, and the UN find themselves under attack by a president who dismisses them as either useless or malicious. For a multilateralist like Justin Trudeau, the problem will be standing up for such institutions while trying to remain in the Trump government's favour.

Finally, personality may itself be a challenge. On the international stage, Trudeau has been framed as an inspiring figure, the personification of a new generation of hope and promise.

Trump, on the other hand, has been positioned as a throwback to a time when America was meaner, smaller, more insular and selfish.

Should that narrative take hold, Trudeau will risk developing an adversarial relationship with a president who has demonstrated time and again that he not only has a fragile ego coupled with a narcissistic personality, but he takes up all the available oxygen in a room.

The Trudeau government has navigated the challenges well thus far, but a Trump presidency fundamentally alters the waters. No longer are we in an age of North American liberal ascendancy; instead, many of the underpinnings of such an agenda are under direct attack.

The ability to adjust to real-life circumstances while keeping strategic focus is at the core of the challenge of governing. In 2009, Stephen Harper and Jim Flaherty, elected on—and believing in—a platform of strict fiscal conservatism, found themselves deciding to run a deficit. They adapted to circumstance for the good of the country. Whether Trudeau can do the same may decide the fate of his government in 2019.

Justin Trudeau's government, along with most Canadians, received quite a shock when they learned in November 2016 that the man they previously knew only as a reality television personality would assume the reins of that metaphorical sleeping elephant. We were reminded of one of politics' most enduring truths: there is no such thing as a guarantee. As post-election uncertainty reigned, pundits argued it every which way. Some prophesied Trump would ring in the apocalypse, others lampooned what they saw as gross overreactions. But no matter where you stood, most felt Trump would be a consequential president for Canada's national future. And so he was. But not in all the ways you might expect.

Facing Trump's presidency, I predicted Trudeau would face challenges on three main fronts: on environmental policy, foreign policy, and personality. Challenges these were. Trump's attack on carbon pricing helped cement a resistance to the idea that remains to this day. The protracted NAFTA renegotiation insisted upon by Trump (after classifying the standing agreement as the "worst trade deal ever made"[31]) was, of course, a constant headache for the Liberal government. And finally, after initial neighbourly niceties, let us not forget how the formal relationship between the two ended. Trump deemed Trudeau "two-faced" and a "far-left lunatic." Ouch.

And yet, no matter how daunting the challenges Trump presented became, they could never outweigh the singularly effective tactic his presidency afforded the Liberals: the ability to cast Trump as Trudeau's natural foil, as a harbinger of what could befall us here should we elect a right-wing government ourselves. However ludicrous it might now sound, the truth is this strategy worked. And because the American media circus never stopped, that tactic remained relevant. In this way, the prime minister did what only the best politicians can do: transform a negative into a positive. When the history books are written, this will surely be counted as a triumph for Trudeau. Why? Because, just as the column calls for, he adapted to circumstances for the good of the country.

February 19, 2017

By focusing on the centre, Trudeau has cleared space for a New Democratic Party that at one point looked lost. The 2019 incarnation of the New Democratic Party should not resemble the centre-left, anti-deficit, pro-business party that was pitched to Canadians in 2015.

Trudeau Has Created an Opening for the NDP

Times have been tough for the federal New Democrats. They entered the 2015 election as contenders for the big prize but, as a result of a series of unfortunate decisions, on election day voters returned them to their traditional third-party role.

It didn't take long for many New Democrats to publicly denounce their leader. The result was as inevitable as it was predictable: polls reported the party found itself, for a time, within the margin of error of the Green Party.

And like seven-year-olds playing soccer, pundits, as a whole, rushed to write the party off.

However, it would appear NDP fortunes are starting to change. The party's leadership campaign is gaining media attention, high-profile leadership candidates are beginning to emerge, and its polling numbers may, just may, finally be turning around.

At the same time, the Liberal government also appears to be turning a corner. Prime Minister Justin Trudeau's recent difficulties—including the bungled electoral reform promise, the cash-for-access scandal, and the fallout in provincial relations over health care—have begun to disappear from the front pages.

The prime minister is once again making headlines for his savvy in international relations.

Many feared Trudeau would not match up well with US president Donald Trump, someone who is brash, self-interested, and easily offended. However, after Monday's unremarkable and conventional meeting in Washington, Trump gave his word that Canada's historic relationship with the United States would only become stronger. Monday's meeting could not have gone better for Trudeau and for Canada; it was a performance the entire country should applaud.

Add to this, a series of smaller victories: Canada added 48,300 jobs to the economy in January, dropping the national unemployment rate to 6.8 percent. In Quebec, Trudeau delivered on his promise to assist Bombardier. And in the coming weeks, he will announce a series of infrastructure projects, marijuana legislation that will rally and excite the millennial base, and progress on the Keystone XL Pipeline that will appeal to moderates in Alberta.

The Liberal Party clearly has a firm grip on the centre of the political spectrum. In recent times, this could be counted as a political victory. However, in today's political climate, moderation is viewed as the elitist status quo. Centrists are often viewed as indecisive on the big issues of the day and indifferent to the plight of ordinary people. Internationally, centrist political parties have had little electoral success of late. Instead, it is candidates and leaders on the fringes who have gained political steam and attention.

By focusing on the centre, Trudeau has cleared space for a New Democratic Party that at one point looked lost. Trudeau's policies and decisions—his enthusiasm for pipelines, embrace of Harper-era greenhouse-gas emission targets, perceived failures on improving the lives of Indigenous Canadians, and cynical abandonment of electoral reform—have given the New Democrats the lifeline they needed.

The 2019 incarnation of the New Democratic Party should not resemble the centre-left, anti-deficit, pro-business party that was pitched to Canadians in 2015.

Rather, the NDP should select a protest candidate who will invigorate the Left and stand as a stark contrast to the current prime minister.

Regardless of who becomes the next leader of the federal NDP—whether it is Charlie Angus, the hard-working, well-liked, Northern Ontario MP; Peter Julian, the anti-pipeline 99 percenter, or Jagmeet Singh, the *GQ*-featured, suburban-whisperer Ontario MPP—they will be free to seize the space on the left and rebuild their party.

Federal politics in Canada has been a race to the centre for a long time. As a result, Canadians have bemoaned their lack of genuine political choice. Everyone understood that while the colour of the drapes might change, that no matter who occupied 24 Sussex Drive, the fundamentals of life in Canada would be relatively unchanged.

In the 2019 election, this theory will be tested. Will Canadians, like voters around the world, vote for a candidate who panders to the far right or left, or will they opt for one who owns the middle ground?

Trudeau is betting on history—a history that favours the Canadian way, that favours that glorious promise of peace, order, and good government.

I think Canadians likely will too.

LIMITED PERSPECTIVE

When I wrote this piece in 2017, it seemed that Canadian centrism might soon become a thing of the past. The election of Donald Trump and the rise of far-right parties in Europe pointed to a future where Justin Trudeau's bet on classical Canadian centrism to win the 2019 election was ill-advised. It therefore seemed logical to wager that the NDP would move from the centrist days of Layton toward a left-wing future. A future where it was imagined that they would be welcomed into the loving arms of a Canadian public awaiting them there.

This series of events was proven to be only half-correct. With the election of Jagmeet Singh as leader, the NDP did follow the yellow brick road left. Standing in contrast to Trudeau, the Singh NDP embraced raising taxes on the wealthy and increased investment in green energy and police reform.

No matter how loudly the NDP sang, however, they could not entice the Canadian public to follow them to the promised land of a socialist Oz. In both the 2019 and 2021 federal elections, Canadians overwhelmingly kept toward the centre, voting to keep the Liberals in power. As Trudeau's gamble paid off, the NDP were left with plenty of rhetoric but minimal results.

What I should have discussed—in predicting that the NDP would challenge the Liberals—was, ironically, the implications that flowed from one of Trudeau's most infamous reneged promises: electoral reform. In our first-past-the-post system, strategic voting remains widespread. So, while there may have been a shift to the left amongst Canadian voters, it's clear many chose what they saw as the lesser evil as opposed to the possibility of a greater good. And of course, the Liberals dutifully played their part to encourage this behaviour, issuing apocalyptic warnings about what would happen if the Conservatives seized power. That strategy worked, and the NDP's dreams were left in Kansas. Ultimately, I should have foreseen that one of Trudeau's broken promises would help him both to extend his tenure as prime minister and prove the NDP's far-left pivot to be a disastrous one.

The embattled Ontario premier believes she is doing the best for the people of the province and so does her team. They think they can win and she isn't going away, regardless of poor poll results.

It's Foolish to Count Kathleen Wynne Out

K athleen Wynne is not going anywhere.

And that's for one very good reason—the premier truly believes she has a shot at victory.

In recent months, speculation about her possible departure as Ontario premier has increased. Yet, as the provincial election looms next year, Wynne has repeatedly insisted she is here to stay.

This insistence comes in spite of increasing concern among Liberals that her unpopularity is hurting the party. That anxiety is not entirely misplaced.

A recent Forum Research poll had the Ontario Liberals in third place, expected to receive about 19 percent of the provincial vote. This was nearly twenty-four points behind the Progressive Conservatives and ten points behind the NDP.

With numbers like this, a Liberal victory looks far out of reach.

However, no one should count Wynne out. She is a strong campaigner and an effective communicator. She is capable and incredibly hard-working. The biggest mistake the Progressive Conservatives can make is to forget about Wynne's potential as a candidate.

The premier has begun to lay out her game plan for victory. She will pursue an aggressive and progressive policy agenda in a bid to capture enough progressive centrist and left-leaning votes to defeat both the Progressive Conservatives and the NDP. Her initiatives will move government to the left—far left.

So, what is her path to victory?

First, the premier has announced measures to try to temper skyrocketing home prices, a move that will resonate with many voters and help secure support on the left.

Second, expect the premier to announce that the minimum wage will increase to fifteen dollars an hour by 2018.

Third, she will announce a guaranteed annual income program for low-wage workers and welfare recipients. This will win her back some support among middle-class workers who feel this government has largely ignored their concerns about jobs and the economy.

And fourth, next winter, Wynne is banking on Ontarians being happy to see that their hydro bills have decreased by 25 percent from the previous winter.

The premier has a few other things going for her.

Wynne has Prime Minister Justin Trudeau in her corner, and he has proven to be an effective resource for Liberals in provincial elections across the country. The Liberal brand remains very strong in Ontario.

With that said, do I think Wynne can win? Only a fool could be goaded into answering that question.

But do I think she believes she can win? Do I think her team believes they can win with her? One hundred percent.

There is a comparable example in recent Canadian political history—none other than Wynne's nemesis, former prime minister Stephen Harper.

Both defied the odds to win majority governments (Harper in 2011 and Wynne in 2014), and both, despite daunting polls, decided they were the best people to lead their parties one last time.

The premier and her supporters staunchly believe that the work her party is doing is for the good of the province and the people of Ontario. Harper's supporters also had faith that the work he was doing was critical for the nation. Among supporters, Wynne has thus far been given as wide a berth as Harper had in the run-up to his failed re-election.

But what about those terrible polls?

Wynne will almost certainly have a better 2017-2018 than 2016-2017, but the hurdle she needs to overcome may be insurmountable.

One thing, though: political polls have lately not been especially accurate indicators of election outcomes, as we saw south of the border in November.

Perhaps Wynne believes Ontario voters simply have a case of "Liberal fatigue"—the party has been the government in Ontario since 2003—that they will get over at election time.

What's more, while Ontarians may not like the current direction of the province, the other parties haven't offered anything else yet.

Hers is not an easy road to victory, and Wynne, experienced political leader that she is, undoubtedly knows this.

But as long as she continues to believe she is doing the right thing for Ontario, and as long as she is doing it from behind the premier's desk, it is not surprising that she has not stepped aside. No one should count on her doing so.

YIKES...

The gas-plants scandal. Surging hydro bills. Fifteen fatiguing years of Liberal rule. Kathleen Wynne carried all this with her in the lead-up to the 2018 Ontario provincial election. Then, in an unprecedented move, the weekend *before* that 2018 election—the results already painfully clear—Wynne conceded in an attempt to persuade voters to still vote Liberal.

Her party suffered devastating results regardless. The Ontario Liberals were crushed, winning just seven seats (Wynne, ever the fighter, still won her riding), while Doug Ford triumphed with a commanding majority.[32] It was a result reminiscent of the fate of their federal cousins when they were reduced to third-party status in 2011.

Now that Wynne's political career has concluded, we must remember how the 2014 victory that won her the premiership was not only surprising but also defied all the normal political calculus. She led a government long in the tooth, a ship primed to go down. (Maybe there is, after all, something to the idea that women leaders are often elected in the most desperate of circumstances.) And yet, there was another equation at play: that of page-turning politics.

In their 2013 leadership race, the Ontario Liberals made a sage choice in choosing Wynne, because it helped the party show Ontarians that the Libs had something new to offer. In the useful shorthand of politics, a gay woman replaced a straight white male.

The thing about "page turners"? There's always another page—a more refreshing alternative that can capture the electorate's favour. In this case, the call was for a fresh face outside the party. And just as Wynne was a successful page-turner when she won her leadership contest, so too was Doug Ford after he won the Ontario PC leadership (helping the party turn the page from Patrick Brown).

In the end, Wynne stood no chance. But as the first openly gay premier in Canada, her political legacy lives on both as a shining example of service before self and an inspiration to all who are told politics is not for them.

October 21, 2018

On the marijuana file, despite many challenges, the federal Liberals forecast exceptionally well and have earned political capital with a year to go before the next election.

Pot Legalization a Lesson in Savvy Political Timing

In politics, there are two factors—over which you have no control—that determine your fate: timing and luck.

In running for office, Prime Minister Justin Trudeau seems to have taken his father's advice that "the essential ingredient of politics is timing" to heart. Promises, which were the foundation of his 2015 campaign, were each cleverly timed to catch the changing mood of Canadians.

A tax cut for the middle class and those aspiring to join it, deficit spending to fund renewal of our aging infrastructure, the welcoming of twenty-five thousand Syrian refugees, and the legalization of marijuana. All were easy to promise at a campaign stop. Each would have its difficulties and obstacles when it came to implementation.

In particular, the legalization of marijuana, an issue that at first blush seemed straightforward turned out to be, upon deeper inspection, fraught with challenges.

But on the marijuana file, in spite of those challenges, the Liberals forecast exceptionally well.

Political capital is, after all, fleeting. The view of voters, at best, unstable. Those on top one day can find themselves at the bottom just a year later.

That's why leaders try to use timing to beat the need for luck. That's why prime ministers often try to accomplish their most challenging political objectives at the start of their mandates.

Trudeau's Liberals knew they needed to have legalization sorted before 2019. They also knew they had a better chance to bring skittish Canadians along if they did so before the government got into the nitty-gritty business of cannabis.

By starting down this road early, the Liberals were able to establish a thoughtful process for legalization: they afforded significant time for consultation with business, third-party organizations, and the provinces. The result was that they were able to accomplish their goal with a year to spare before the next election.

By October 17, the day pot became legal, this endlessly talked-about, "earth-shattering" moment in Canadian politics unfolded as just another dry day in the House of Commons. Conservative leader Andrew Scheer did not even mention legalization during Question Period that day.

The Liberals know, however, that a chunk of Canadians remain firmly against their policy initiative. To mitigate the electoral impact of this, the Liberals are counting on voters to have become distracted by other issues of a new day.

And what about the 30 percent of Canadians who enjoy marijuana regularly? Here the Liberals hope they will be rewarded for legalizing cannabis when these voters get to the ballot box.

But timing isn't the only thing. When asked what the toughest challenge to his administration was, Harold Macmillan, the former prime minister of the United Kingdom, replied, "Events, dear boy, events." And this is where luck comes into play. American football great Vince Lombardi once said, "Luck is what happens when preparation meets opportunity."

And the Liberals found themselves with no shortage of luck on this file.

At the time of his election in 2015, Trudeau faced a very different slate of premiers than he does today. Then, more than 80 percent of Canadians lived in a province with a progressive-leaning premier who favoured legalization.

Since that time, the political climate in the provinces has changed dramatically and, if the pollsters are correct in Alberta, will continue to change.

The prime minister faced very little scrutiny from the provinces regarding marijuana when he launched his initiative. Manitoba was the only jurisdiction that attempted to derail the legalization process.

More recently, however, premiers who have grown united against Trudeau on several other policy files have begun to make noise about challenges to the rollout of marijuana legalization and the federal government's supervision (or lack thereof) of the process.

Ontario's premier, Doug Ford, fired his first warning shot on Wednesday. Don't expect it to be his last.

Imagine if Ford had been there since the beginning, rallying those Canadians who opposed the legalization—and pointing out the flaws in the Liberal plans.

Timing or luck? Why choose?

I can vividly remember the strong reactions to Justin Trudeau's announcement in the opening days of the famed 2015 federal election that he would, if elected, legalize marijuana.

To put into context just how bold this promise was (and therefore how effective it would prove to be), not even Tom Mulcair's NDP had, at that point, committed to a step so daring. It was a high-risk, high-reward play to call—but just the kind of thing that can springboard a party from third place to first.

At the time, several conservative friends of mine summarized Trudeau's proclamation as nothing more than a dream. But it's these exact cases, where perceived dreams (such as equal marriage in 2005 or the Canadian Human Rights Act in 1977) turn out to be reality, that are worth closely examining.

While I was right that the success of this policy was a combination of savvy political timing and luck, I should have probed deeper.

Precisely because many Canadians dismissed this issue as an outright dream was the promise so politically advantageous for Trudeau. Even in 2015, you did not need extensive polling to tell you a generational divide was at play. Young Canadians who had just become of age to vote believed strongly in legalization and were willing to express that view at the ballot box. Thus, when Trudeau picked up this torch, it was not a shock for that younger generation but instead a relief that a political leader had *finally* tapped into something they cared about.

The truth today seems painfully apparent: marijuana legalization was an issue *just waiting* for a party with the courage to pick it up and benefit from the popularity it held. Politicians—opposition leaders especially—should be searching for today's equivalent of marijuana legalization. There is no shortage of potentially revolutionary ideas that, as events here revealed, can transform political fortunes.

May 19, 2019

What was clearly Trudeau's greatest asset in 2015
may well be his undoing in 2019.

The Gift of Social Media
Helped Trudeau, But It
Can Also Take Away

When Justin Trudeau took the stage in October 2015 to celebrate the Liberals' majority victory, he spoke of his party's
"positive vision" for Canada.

Their campaign, he said, had "defeated the idea that Canadians should
be satisfied with less, that good enough is good enough and that better just
isn't possible . . . this is Canada, and in Canada better is always possible."

As we head into what may well be one of the closest and most
unpredictable election campaigns in recent years, his words that night
could not be more prescient. This *is* Canada—and, especially in an election
year, Canadians will be looking for something better from their politics.

Four years ago, polling showed that two-thirds of Canadians wanted
a change in government. And it was that longing for something new, not
just in policy but in style and approach, that Trudeau's team so effectively
harnessed and rode to their majority.

Their "real change" platform explicitly laid out the contrast between
Tory present and Liberal future. Stephen Harper, on the other hand, concluded his foreword to the Conservative platform by claiming his Economic

Action Plan was a success. "It's working," he said. "Let's continue on with what we know works."

In attack ads and campaign messaging, the Tories characterized Trudeau's "celebrity" appearance—and especially his hair—as proof of style over substance. On social media, the Liberals responded by claiming that he had both and did so in a way that was charming, pithy, and most importantly, *viral*.

From the new-found power of Instagram to the traditionally influential pages of *Vogue*, the prime minister managed to capture the attention of the digital age in a way few politicians, Canadian or otherwise, had.

And it worked. Trudeau came to be deemed Obama's successor as the leader of the world's progressives.

But what was clearly Trudeau's greatest asset in 2015 may well be his undoing in 2019.

The problem with a campaign built on self-image and the optics of virtue is that people, inconveniently, expect it to be true. And what is fairly easy to execute in a campaign setting becomes near impossible to implement when governing.

What's more, the gift social media gives, it also takes away. Unlike campaign advertising or stump speeches—which Canadians know are contrived—the power of social media lies in the sense that what you are seeing is, at least to some extent, genuine.

And so, when Canadians see their PM beaming with pride over his gender-balanced cabinet or taking a selfie with a young couple while out for a jog, style becomes conflated with substance.

And now, after four years of governing, that conflation has become a collision. The chickens have come home to roost. In short, Trudeau is paying the price of the expectations he set when he promised to be a new and different kind of leader and began to practice the politics of political celebrity.

By dubbing himself the "feminist prime minister," Trudeau opened himself up to the attacks that inevitably followed his expulsion of Jody Wilson-Raybould and Jane Philpott from his caucus.

In trumpeting his commitment to Indigenous communities—not least of which being a visit to a teepee set up by activists on Parliament Hill—

Trudeau set himself up to be pilloried not only for his slow progress on Indigenous files but for tone-deaf responses to Indigenous protestors.

And by claiming the mantle of Canada's traditionally welcoming stance on immigration as his own, he has made himself vulnerable to the attacks of challengers who want to paint him as responsible for what they characterize as an unsustainable influx of irregular border crossers.

Many believe governments are not defeated, but rather that they defeat themselves. On the whole, I disagree. I think, in most cases, governments are elected to do a particular job, and when that job is done, another party is called up to bat.

For Trudeau, the job he was hired to do was to bring, in his own words, sunny ways to government.

Now that is done, Trudeau's challenge is to rewrite his job description in a way that convinces Canadians he still has work to do and is still the best leader for the job.

FAULTY WIRING

Almost a decade on from Justin Trudeau's seismic 2015 win, the image of the old-fashioned Conservative wholly ignorant of social media's utility no longer carries water. Indeed, both Doug Ford and Pierre Poilievre have used it to impressive effect.

Now that the battlefield is level, mastery of this domain is likely to be a determinant of success.

In this column, I forewarn that Trudeau's social media popularity could be his downfall. My argument is premised on the assumption that social media's power lies in its appearance of authenticity. I claim Canadians *expect* traditional campaigns to be a space of contrivance, whereas they expect what they see on social media to reflect reality. Time has proven this to be manifestly, undeniably false.

What's the solution? Obviously, there are no easy answers, but here are two places we can start.

First is to continue calling out hypocrisy. There is no better way to combat an imposter than to remove their mask. Mercifully, social media offers numerous means to do just that.

Second, we should turn to those with the most experience on these platforms for guidance—young people. These Canadians have learned about the negatives of social media from an early age. They know more about its methods of duplicity and deceit than many of us could ever hope to. Leaving the health of our democratic institutions to those who can't tell an iPhone from an Android will almost certainly doom us.

With the help of our younger generations, who have the most to lose, we must find ways to ensure that new media is a means to uproot and challenge political artifice, not simply strengthen it.

If Canadians feel that someone has made a mistake for which they are genuinely contrite, they have an astounding capacity for forgiveness. The key to that forgiveness, however, lies in the word "genuine."

Justin Trudeau Can Earn Forgiveness, But He Will Have to Continually Work to Earn It

This week, the federal election campaign was thrown into chaos when years-old pictures emerged of Justin Trudeau dressed up in a way most would deem highly inappropriate.

Commentators around the country, indeed around the world, have weighed in with comments on the prime minister's conduct and the sincerity of his apologies.

For a country that all too often rests on its laurels when it comes to issues of discrimination and race, it is an important conversation to have. We like to smugly contrast ourselves favourably with our southern neighbours and sing the praises of our multicultural society.

We hear it all the time: "Canada is a mosaic, not a melting pot," and "Toronto is the most multicultural city in the world."

Well, yes, but that multiculturalism did not come without a price paid by many Canadians—especially racialized and Indigenous groups—who still face prejudice every day of their lives.

Their experiences are their own and not only do I not presume to speak on their behalf, I can't. As a gay man, I can, however, share some of the pain and humiliation of having had to endure painful and haunting episodes of discrimination in my own life. It is about more than political correctness—it is about lived experience.

So, when I first saw those images on Wednesday evening, I was of course taken aback. Sitting at dinner with my colleagues, I began to wonder, "How will the prime minister respond to this? Will Canadians ever forgive him?"

Forgiveness in the public sphere need not be a complicated thing. Over the course of my career, I have had the privilege to meet with and learn from Canadians, literally, from all walks of life. And I have come to learn just how decent and understanding they are. If Canadians feel that someone has made a mistake for which they are genuinely contrite, they have an astounding capacity for forgiveness.

The key to that forgiveness, however, lies in the word "genuine." A sense of authentic penitence is the essential starting point of public reconciliation. Without it, an apology is not worth the paper on which it's written.

But there is more. The apology itself matters. A lot. Trudeau's hasty apology on Wednesday night missed the mark. His focus was on himself. Not on those he hurt and harmed.

On Thursday, Trudeau tried again. And this time he got it right.

"I was blind," he said, "to the pain that I may have caused at those times and that I am now causing to people that count on me to defend them." He spoke as someone who understood he had made a mistake. As a man who deeply regretted his actions and had only recently come to understand their significance.

Time will tell whether this incident has shifted the dial of his electoral fate.

Asked why he should be allowed to stay in office, I was struck by the Liberal leader's response: "I'm going to be asking Canadians to forgive me for what I did."

His answer stood in stark contrast to his unequivocal non-apologies in the SNC-Lavalin affair and it spoke to a comprehension of the severity of his actions.

But what does it really mean for Canadians to forgive a public figure?

In a practical sense, forgiveness at the polls would mean allowing Trudeau to return to Ottawa and begin, in earnest, to reconcile the hurt he has inflicted.

On a deeper level, the prime minister may wish for Canadians to view his past transgressions as the starting point of his transformation into a devoted public servant.

Is it not a testament to his "different" vision for Canadian politics that the obliviously ignorant man in those photos could, twenty years later, become a champion for the rights of minorities and the oppressed?

Forgiveness is a journey and Trudeau will have to continue working to prove that those photos do not represent the man who wants to be our prime minister today.

The process will be drawn-out, uncomfortable and, at times, painful. Perhaps that is a fitting penance, given the very real pain that has been caused.

MISSED THE MARK

Suffice it to say, Canadians have heard Justin Trudeau apologize more than enough times throughout his tenure. He's issued long-overdue formal apologies on behalf of the Government of Canada for historical shortcomings and crimes. He's also made myriad personal apologies, especially for past conduct—as was the case here.

When this photo came out, many people thought the PM was toast. But it would be deeply naive to state that Canadians *have* forgiven Trudeau by granting him victories in 2019 and 2021. Indeed, upon reflection, I feel it's unproductive to probe this topic in purely political terms. It's simply the wrong lens.

In a climate where people have more to apologize for (both justifiably and not), the practice and culture of apology is losing coherence. There is no clear compass to find that sense of genuineness I praise.

Let's reverse the equation. What is an apology—be it a grand speech or a bottle of wine for your next-door neighbour—*trying* to achieve? Answer: forgiveness. It's one of our highest public virtues. If it ceases to mean anything, it's not helpful.

But forgiveness is a choice. So my question, "What does it mean for Canadians to forgive a public figure?" is based on a false premise. If the criteria for what constitutes a successful apology for public figures differs vastly from what we expect from our friends or family, our ailing culture of apology won't get any better. No. These criteria must instead be, as far as possible, *the same.*

Perspectives on what makes a successful apology will never be conveniently uniform. And yet, most of us share in the desire not merely for words but for action. True remorse must be accompanied by demonstrable change.

This is where we let our public figures off the hook. We cannot be satisfied by poetic expressions of regret. We must instead focus on making it known which course of action can make things right.

July 25, 2022

History teaches that large majority governments,
particularly those without effective opposition,
can quickly sow the seeds of their eventual defeat.

Cautionary Tales for Doug Ford's Progressive Conservatives on the Unseen Dangers of Majority Rule

I t's the stuff political dreams are made of.

A resounding mandate born of a strategic and methodical campaign. A headless opposition—divided in allegiance, confused in direction, adrift. A feeling, perhaps even a certainty, that it is the very best of times. And yet, in the political world, it takes precious little for the dream to spoil and the tale to turn cautionary.

For Ontario's recently re-elected Progressive Conservative government to avoid such a fate and to maintain the confidence of its electorate, they must be wary of the pitfalls that have befallen past governments in similar, seemingly unassailable positions.

Doing so is simple but not easy. It requires the exercise of an uncommon level of vigilance to combat the tendencies of arrogance and recklessness that so often accompany major political victories. History teaches that large majority governments, particularly those without effective partisan opposition, are prone to the miscalculations that quickly sow the seeds of their eventual defeat.

For evidence, Premier Doug Ford's government need look no further than the fate of their federal cousins after the infamous 1988 "free-trade election."[33] With a victory that the *New York Times* characterized as a "stunning reversal" in their front page headline the next day, former prime minister Brian Mulroney's win could not have been sweeter. With that majority in hand and the two main opposition parties leaderless, the quest to build a free-trade market across the forty-ninth parallel lay open. And yet, only five short years later, the federal Progressive Conservative Party was reduced to two seats—in other words, rubble.

The greater the triumph, the greater the fall.

In crises, the deadliest poison is hubris—and along with it, a sense of invincibility, a failure to anticipate adversity and to plan long-term. Second-term majority governments often fall into this trap when they abandon not only the principles but the very political acuity that won them their power.

During its first term, the Ford government proved highly responsive to public opinion, demonstrating a willingness to make concessions and reverse course on several key issues, including its response to the pandemic. This dexterity—some would say humility—surprised many, and in Ford's view, significantly contributed to his party's re-election.

But that was then. Today, the premier and his government face the daunting dual challenges of ballooning inflation and a looming recession—circumstances that will require the government to be more politically adept than ever. For example, research by our firm Navigator found that three-quarters of Ontarians are convinced the provincial government can act to tame inflation, ascribing more tools to the government than they actually have.

Into the expanding bag of issues, throw gas prices, an overburdened health-care system, and the rising challenge of affordability. Add to it the risk of a media that will be emboldened and increasingly hostile given the lack of an effective opposition, and before you know it, a bunker mentality will set in. It happens all the time in second-term governments, and it will take relentless discipline to prevent it.

The best recipe to avoid the worst of times is for the Ford government to ignore the happy circumstance of a weak opposition, instead employing the same political calculus that has been essential to their triumphs thus far. One that has been wedded both to the guidance of public opinion, yet at the same time resilient to strong criticism.

The simple fact is that this government won a larger majority with fewer votes. As history shows, it's a victory that could turn to a crushing defeat in four short years without restraint, a clear vision and an appetite to solve once-in-a-lifetime challenges.

The opening weeks of a rare summertime sitting of Ontario's legislature at the "Pink Palace" will provide the first clue as to how much heed they will pay to the cautionary lessons of those majorities past, once seemingly indestructible.

GOOD BONES

Most political wisdom is versatile enough to be applied in situations of either opposition or government. But there's a crucial, rarer form that comes only from the experience of governing. It can only be acquired, fully understood, and appreciated, through the drama, struggle, and mysteries of governing. My warning here to Doug Ford is of just this kind, and it remains essential that he heed it.

Today the Ford government is making the very decisions that I warned about, decisions that will come back to haunt them. Simply telling this cautionary tale through historical events, as I did with the fall of Brian Mulroney's government, is not forceful enough.

Here's what I should have said: Over their second term in office, Doug Ford and the Ontario PCs will be in a long-distance car race with their political opponents from Windsor to Thunder Bay. In winning a second-term majority government, they have secured a sizable head start. If they heed the lessons of history, they should not speed out of the gate by attempting to force through legislation that is unpopular even with the voters who elected them. Nor should they take needless shortcuts, like using the notwithstanding clause as if it's a commonplace tool, as they have three times since 2018.[34] Such actions risk wearing out the tires and suspension. The journey is long; they should frequently pause along their voyage to check in on their supporters. They cannot afford to just drive on past.

Soon enough, the NDPs and Liberals will have flashy new cars with little mileage. In the closing days of the race, if the Conservative vehicle is sufficiently battered, their competitors might be able to catch up and overtake.

On the other hand, slow and steady, responsive and disciplined, will help secure a win in 2026.

Hurried and wayward, mindless and uncontrolled, will leave Ontarians hungry for a change.

January 5, 2023

Throughout our country, we must not allow our politics to continue being—as Orwell described it—"the choice between the lesser of two evils."

In 2023, Canadians Deserve a Grand Vision from Our Political Leaders

A federal election in 2023?

Though far from a certainty, more and more, it feels like one. Federal minority governments have seldom endured more than a few years and the current Liberal-NDP agreement is unlikely to be an exception to this rule.

If the plug is pulled and the current Parliament Hill tone continues, the election will be waged on decidedly pessimistic terms. Take, for example, Conservative leader Pierre Poilievre's and Prime Minister Justin Trudeau's recent exchange played out over the closing weeks of 2022.

To great effect, Poilievre has repeatedly asserted that "it feels like everything is broken in this country"—a message that resonates strongly with Canadians. At a year-end Liberal holiday party, Trudeau countered that "Canada is not broken."

While Canada is far from broken, it's time we acknowledged that there are significant cracks in the land, and the current government's continued approach of ignoring the legitimate concerns of families battling record inflation and a housing crisis can't continue.

As Poilievre tells it, Justin Trudeau's excessive spending, runaway deficits, and second-rate commitment to infrastructure mean that a continued Liberal reign poses no less than an existential threat to our nation.

Trudeau's challenge is that circumstances beyond his control—namely brutal economic conditions—make defending against Poilievre's charges harder and harder. He is left, as many long-term governments are, selling a hypothetical alternative narrative of another kind of doom and gloom.

And so, Trudeau paints a sloppy picture of a Poilievre-inspired hellscape where you pay for groceries with Ethereum and carbon costs less than an FTX token. Put a pox on both their houses on this one. Better than cartoonish imaginings, our politics requires, now more than in a long time, great causes and long-term objectives. Nothing places this fact into more apparent relief than immigration.

The Liberal's target of welcoming 465,000 permanent residents in 2023, 485,000 in 2024, and five hundred thousand in 2025 is an important objective. Laudable for its human compassion and much needed for the future strength of our economy.

That said, we need to be ready to welcome these newcomers with, among other things, affordable housing and reliable, accessible health care. The Trudeau government still needs to provide something close to a realistic plan. So far, its approach has been painfully insufficient.

Of course, grand visions amount to very little if they are unaccompanied by concrete plans and dedicated action. Historically, there is no better marriage of these two criteria than the revolutionary New Deal. During a rousing speech to the Democratic National Convention in 1936, the man behind it, President Franklin D. Roosevelt asserted, "This generation of Americans has a rendezvous with destiny." He spoke these words while his nation was still caught in the grasp of the world's most significant economic collapse, five years before it entered its most crucial conflict.

As we awaken in 2023, our challenge—Canadians and our political leaders alike—will be to rally around many of the same appointments: one grand vision, concrete plans, and a dedication to action.

Backward glances into the trials of COVID-19 will do us little good. Instead, meeting such a challenge requires us to rethink and revamp our social, technological, and economic policies. It demands that we ask and answer determining questions: Should we expand our global influence or turn inward? Do we still need a monarchy? Which industries will define our future? What, as a nation, is our greatest priority?

Throughout our country, we must not allow our politics to continue being—as Orwell described it—"the choice between the lesser of two evils." Canadians deserve a grand vision. Unfortunately, we've suffered without it for far too long.

AGED LIKE MILK

A couple of things about this column.

First, I'm not sure if I was just high on life or high on something else, but I have no idea why I said that a federal election in 2023 looked likely. That idea doesn't make any sense. For the prime minister to trigger one would be an act of such calculating and nakedly apparent self-interest that the public would surely punish him. Why? Well, for playing electoral games, for one. And for neglecting the serious issues crippling families countrywide.

Every sensible commentator agrees that the next election will be a hyper-partisan, divisive contest. A binary choice. The New Democrats would be signing their own death warrant if they were to defeat the government.

So that's that.

Now, onto the column itself and this idea that it is time for a grand national vision.

It is.

And it is especially necessary given our commitment to start welcoming five hundred thousand immigrants yearly by 2025.[35]

Politicians can, and will, skirmish around the issues of the day. But those debates only take us so far. Long ago, Sir Wilfred Laurier, Canada's seventh prime minister, said that "the twentieth century shall be the century of Canada."[36]

Now what? What does Canada's future look like? What are we going to commit ourselves to?

As we have seen, the answer is not one we can leave to the politicians to divine. In fact, we'd be fools if we waited for them. Let's not forget that our political system militates against transformation.

Rather, it is time we got to work and did it ourselves. It is time for us to have that great national conversation—much talked about but not yet initiated.

When we do, can we ground it in something other than hopelessness and despair? Let's undertake the discussion with the fundamental belief that this is a great country, one with a rich history of punching well above its weight, with a population that is one of the most diverse in the world, and with natural resources that are the envy of many.

4

In Opposition

The Waiting Room

They say your worst day in government is better than your best day in opposition.

Why's that, you might ask?

Because at least on a bad day in government, you still have the keys to the joint.

Let's face it, most people who go into politics do so because they want to be in charge. They may want to fix things. Improve their communities. Right wrongs. Get the bad guys. Extend a hand to the people life has been especially shitty to. But along with all these noble desires, many politicians also have an ego that says, "I can fix that." And so whether it comes to improving local public transportation or revitalizing health-care services nationwide, the truth is we need community leaders with an ego large enough to allow them to step up to the plate and be fearless enough to lead.

And it is these ego-driven instincts that make sitting in opposition so desperately excruciating. The reality of our winner-takes-all system—that it keeps some players so close to the top yet so heartbreakingly far—can be devastating.

In the following columns, I provide insights on the nature of the long, unpredictable race from second (or third) place, and I write about two key areas leaders and parties encounter as they navigate this winding and hazardous course.

The first area looks at the tremendous importance—and distinct pitfalls—of the contests that choose party leaders. Strangely, for all their crucial importance, leadership contests are the one thing parties get wrong as often as they get right. There is a pretty straightforward reason for this: political parties are built for (and have the most experience in) fighting foes on *the outside*, not battles within.

Just as couples in intimate relationships know how to push each other's buttons, party members know how to get a rise out of each other. At best, their fights may resemble an episode of *Family Feud*. At worst, it's a descent into civil war. The challenge, of course, is that when the leadership race is over, those same party members have to put all the simmering feuds behind them, gather around the new leader, and march united into battle against the real opponent. Not always an easy thing to do for the folks who are still licking their wounds or nursing a grudge against someone they thought was one of their very best friends or closest colleagues.

The second area I explore in this section involves the day-to-day challenges that come with serving in opposition, particularly with leading the troops.

It's been said that leading an opposition party is like leading an expedition through the wilderness—with no promise of ever reaching the promised land. Many from within the team will question the charted path, doubting the turns the leader has elected to take. And often, they will do more than just oppose. There will be those who actively work to undermine and even overthrow their leader. In our Westminster system, an opposition leader's primary job is, simply put, to oppose the government in office. Doing so while continuing to appear viable as a future government leader can be extraordinarily challenging. The truth is that opposition leaders represent the unknown. Branding them as unprepared to lead is not only achievable but can be highly effective. I recall the Progressive Conservative Party's war-room success with this tactic when, during the 1999 Ontario provincial election, Mike Harris's campaign declared Dalton McGuinty was "just not up to the job." As a result of ploys like this one, history is full of politicians who were effective opposition leaders but were never able to convince the public they were a mayor, premier, or prime minister *in waiting*.

Governments get to do things. Opposition parties only get to promise things. The longer those promises glimmer just ahead, inert and unfulfilled, the harder it is to maintain enthusiasm with the public and discipline within the team.

But we know that those leaders who can keep it together through these challenges will do better when they win.

Seems we have dress rehearsals for a reason.

March 19, 2017

There will be only one winner with the dream of leading the Conservatives to power. The other thirteen would-be leaders will face the harsh reality of the May 27 leadership vote—and for some it will not be pretty.

Why So Many Candidates Are Still in Race to Lead Tories

E arly last year, I joked that the Conservative leadership race was more like the story of *Snow White and the Seven Dwarfs* than a contest for head of a national party. Today, as more and more would-be leaders jump into the pool, I've come to think of it as the story of *101 Dalmatians*.

The number of entrants is eye-popping; especially for a party that many pundits have assigned a snowball's shot in hell of winning the next election.

Watching the leadership debates—with fourteen participants strolling onto the stage one by one—is like watching a seemingly impossible number of clowns pop out of a Volkswagen Beetle. And the debates themselves don't seem to be debates so much as hours-long question-and-answer snore fests with as little chance of risk, spontaneity, and mistakes as possible.

Indeed, more than once, a few of the leadership contestants have looked perilously close to dozing off during what should be a career-defining event.

The decision to enter a leadership campaign is not one made lightly. It involves raising hundreds of thousands of dollars to campaign non-stop across the country for months.

It's a strain on health, personal finances, and family.

And to top it all off, candidates are competing for a sometimes dubious prize—one that comes with an even more punishing life. A party leader must renew their commitment to non-stop campaigning. In public, that means everything from a strawberry social in Charlottetown to meeting in a church basement in Kelowna.

And within the backrooms of their own party, the new leader has to survive dark rumblings from a caucus desperate to return to power, not all that confident it now has the right leader for the job.

So why have so many Conservatives taken the plunge? It is, after all, a contest that will end in disappointment for thirteen, and an impossibly daunting task for the "lucky" winner.

An observer of US politics once remarked that every morning, 535 members of Congress look at themselves in the mirror and see a future president staring back at them.

The same is true in Canada.

The prospect of leading a party that is but one election cycle away from winning government and launching a new chapter in political history is very tempting for many who have, for years, looked at and listened to Stephen Harper and thought, "I could do better."

That's why, when there's an opening for the leadership of one of the two federal parties in Canada that have formed government, the work begins in earnest.

With major candidates such as John Baird, Peter MacKay, and Jason Kenney absent from the current federal Conservative Party contest, the race becomes even more attractive to other contestants.

The simple fact that there is no clear front-runner with a runaway bandwagon of support means that not one candidate's chances are better than any other's.

The fee to get into the race was a hundred thousand dollars—an amount most members of Parliament and businesspeople who want to enter politics could easily raise. And many will feel that, with so many candidates to split the vote, they have a hope of winning.

But it is an unpleasant fact that thirteen of the contenders will lose. An even more unpleasant fact is that a significant number will lose quite badly, ending with as little as 2 percent of the vote.

Why, then, are they all still in the race? Why haven't some of them dropped out, and spared themselves the embarrassment?

There are a number of reasons.

For many of the fourteen, it is like the first round of a poker game. The have anted up, their money is in, so why not wait and see what happens?

For some, they are running not so much to win this time but more to raise their profile and build their network for a second run against Prime Minister Justin Trudeau.

Others are on a mission to raise the profile of an issue they care deeply about; a good example is Rick Peterson's one-man mission to rid Canada of corporate income tax.

And then, of course, there is yet another reason—vanity.

Many candidates didn't receive this much attention when they were elected to Parliament ten years ago with visions of stars in their eyes. They are flattered by the sustained media and Internet attention.

Many of the fourteen candidates are deluding themselves that they have a chance at winning. Perhaps it's a delusion that can be forgiven, but on May 27 they will face the harsh reality of the results of the leadership vote.

I would wager, however, that several people will wake up the morning of May 28 kicking themselves for having let the glare of attention blind them to the reality of the result.

IN GOOD SHAPE

The Conservative Party of Canada would look quite different today had more party members swung Maxime Bernier's way. But, in the end, Scheer carried the day by just two points.[37]

This contest took place in the wake of a crushing defeat for the Conservatives in the 2015 election. That election saw Stephen Harper, the man who'd rebuilt the party and led them to nearly a decade on the government benches, resign.

As a result, the race had all the ingredients needed for a leadership review on the "soul of the party"—its future and identity. But the dynamic of a successful leader resigning after a long tenure instead occasioned visions of personal glory dancing in each of the heads of a large number of candidates.

And so, as we have seen, it has taken a couple of times for the Conservatives to get things right.

In this first time out in the post-Harper era, the Tories paid a price for this scramble for the spotlight. For me, Scheer represented a vision not of the road ahead but of the rear-view mirror. He was too desirous of the good old days that were never actually as they seemed.

Today, that is replaced with a clear view for what does lie ahead. It's not as if Poilievre doesn't have personal ambition. He does. Nor is it that Poilievre's approach doesn't have the Harper era as part of its DNA. He was, after all, one of the Harper government's most prominent faces. It's rather that Canadians now recognize what the party stands for. Unlike Scheer and Erin O'Toole, Poilievre won his leadership race handily on the first ballot; he did not have to compromise with his opponents to win over their support. His message has been clear and consistent. And now that it's emerged, unfiltered, onto the national stage, that message is resonating with Canadians.

June 4, 2017

The Conservative leadership election has come to a close, but it has opened a new chapter for a party that needed renewal.

Sunny Ways for the Conservative Party

Any party that has served in government faces challenges following an election defeat. Its brand has been buffeted by years of criticism from the opposition parties and from the media. Its players are tired and the recriminations come quickly.

Renewal can be a long and challenging process that takes several election cycles. The situations faced by the federal Liberal Party in 2006 and the Ontario Progressive Conservatives in 2003 show how what seems like a temporary exile can turn into a long stay in the wilderness.

The Conservative Party of Canada has much to celebrate after last weekend.

Through the long leadership campaign, it seemed the party wouldn't have much to rejoice about at the end of it. Media commentators and pundits panned the field of contenders as has-beens or never-weres and dwelled on the fact that major players had opted out of running for the leadership. They panned the policy proposals as uninteresting.

But, today, the Conservative Party finds itself well positioned.

Its already prodigious fundraising has been increasing, even in the midst of a leadership campaign populated by fourteen candidates raising money from the same pool of donors.

Those major players the media called out for staying out of the race have merely gone on to other things. Jason Kenney has moved to Alberta and united the conservative movement there, creating an immediate opportunity for the province to return to the conservative fold in the next election.

John Baird and Peter MacKay have returned to the working world but have signalled their intention to strongly support the party moving forward.

And, more importantly, the candidates that were dismissed as second-tier have demonstrated that they are capable of carrying the mantle forward.

The conservative movement in Canada has a tendency to break at the seams from time to time. The split between the Progressive Conservatives and Reform Party in 1993, and the split in the parties on the right in Alberta are the most recent examples of the fragility of the movement.

Once, a result as close as 50.5 percent to 49.5 percent in a leadership contest would herald, at the very least, increased tensions and frustrations in the party. But party leaders and activists seem to understand the fundamental importance of maintaining a united and strong party to challenge the Liberals if they are to be successful.

The leadership contest brought to the fore fresh faces. A number of MPs who were less than prominent during the Harper era have emerged as important players.

Erin O'Toole, Maxime Bernier, Michael Chong, and a host of other contenders may have lost the leadership election, but they have certainly boosted their profiles. Each can boast that they have shared their perspectives with party members and gained followers. They struggled to emerge from the shadows of the bigger Conservative players in Stephen Harper's government, but they have demonstrated that they are ready and able to help steer the party.

Importantly, Andrew Scheer's election as leader heralds the end of a sometimes cold Conservative Party. Scheer seems intent on reframing his party as one that is positively focused on growth for Canadians. Party members will welcome this tone.

Leadership contests often leave bruised egos and open wounds in their wakes. The aftermath produces periods of introspection and frustration.

None of that has been evident this week.

To the contrary, the new cadre of Conservative frontbenchers seem content with the results and pleased with the direction of the party. There has been none of the usual discontent and grumbling.

Many of the Conservative MPs are newly elected, since generational renewal was a goal of the Harper political machine as it approached the 2015 campaign.

That path was chosen with foresight. Today, the Conservative Party is led by a young leader who is working with a number of promising young MPs and a nearly absurd stockpile of cash.

Sunny ways, indeed!

SWING AND A MISS

I was pretty unequivocal when I proclaimed that, following Scheer's triumph, the Conservative Party was in excellent condition because, for once, it was not plagued by division. That last part was true. In the 2019 election, Scheer and the Conservatives made an impressive comeback (albeit in a losing effort), winning the popular vote by over two hundred thousand votes and gaining twenty-six seats.[38] But I blew it when I failed to identify that to win, they needed to offer Canadian voters something more compelling.

I end this piece by citing Justin Trudeau's "sunny ways" to highlight Scheer's positive outlook, young team, and robust financial backing. Although this slogan may now seem trite, it was the powerful tool that allowed Trudeau to communicate his message of optimism to Canadians and draw a contrast between himself and Stephen Harper.

Scheer lacked this clear branding. Many Canadians struggled not only to identify with him but equally to understand what he stood for. And although, early on, he pledged to bring forward a message of "Conservative positivity," he ran a largely negative campaign in the 2019 federal election.

While praising the Conservative Party for a successful leadership race, I failed to recognize that they were missing a critical ingredient that neither "stockpiles of cash" nor youthful exuberance could buy: a message that resonates with Canadians.

Determining this message is the most challenging decision an opposition party faces. Unlike the party in power, whose choices are more limited because they have a record to defend, opposition parties have much more flexibility. Do they run a "sunny ways" campaign, emphasizing optimism and hope? Or do they run a negative campaign, portraying their party as the only force that can avert impending doom?

This is the central challenge of a campaign strategist. If an opposition party misreads the public sentiment, their campaign won't get out of the gate. Exhibit A: Andrew Scheer.

*On Wednesday night, for the first time, each candidate seemed energized,
on their toes, and unafraid to throw punches. Like a catfish among the cod,
Bloomberg forced his stagemates to eschew their friendly demeanour
and act like the competitors they are.*

Mike Bloomberg Has Woken Up a Sleepy Primary Contest

In his 1913 book *Essays in Rebellion*, British journalist Henry Nevinson illustrated an issue facing the Atlantic fishing trade.

The problem: when shipped in tanks overseas, cod tended to be "lethargic, torpid . . . prone to inactivity, content to lie in comfort . . . rapidly deteriorating in their flesh." The solution, devised by an enterprising fisherman, was to insert one catfish into each tank, ensuring that each cod came to market "firm, brisk, and wholesome . . . for the catfish is the demon of the deep, and keeps things lively."[39]

Nevinson thus introduced the concept of the catfish as a stimulating, corrective presence that forces its neighbouring creatures out of their inertia. Over a hundred years later, the term "catfish" has become a popular expression for social media users who pretend on the Internet to be someone they are not.

Watching the Democratic primary debate this week in Nevada, it became clear that former New York City mayor Mike Bloomberg is, himself, a catfish. Setting aside the unflattering comparison to Nevinson's "demon of the deep," it now looks like Bloomberg's greatest impact as a candidate will be in his capacity to jolt his competitors out of their lethargy. He may not come out on top—characterizing his debate performance as disappointing would be kind—but his candidacy will cull the field and refocus the race.

For months, the Democratic primary has felt underwhelming. Initially framed as a coronation of former vice-president Joe Biden, surprises along the way have culminated in Senator Bernie Sanders' firm dominance in most national polls. Virtually all pundits agree that position will erode as the field narrows to just one or two centrist alternatives to the Vermont senator's staunch socialism.

But the reality is, aside from Sanders' proposed political revolution, none of the candidates has really caught anyone's imagination. Biden seems to have fallen asleep at the wheel, Pete Buttigieg has yet to garner any serious support from crucial minority groups, and Elizabeth Warren's emphasis on substance over style has left voters wondering whether she is up for a general election fight.

But all of that changed on Wednesday night.

For the first time, each candidate seemed energized, on their toes, and unafraid to throw punches. Like a catfish among the cod, Bloomberg forced his stagemates to eschew their friendly demeanour and act like the competitors they are.

Warren came for Bloomberg, Amy Klobuchar swung at Mayor Pete and perhaps most significantly, Sanders learned to defend himself from exactly the kinds of attacks that he would face from Donald Trump.

Responding to Sanders' ardent defence of democratic socialism, Bloomberg noted how "wonderful" the US must be, considering "the best-known socialist in the country happens to be a millionaire with three houses."

Sanders was taken aback. The senator is used to attacks for his socialist views but has yet to experience any serious challenge to the working-class bona fides that have defined his entire political identity. His flustered response shows just how unfamiliar Bloomberg's tactic was. No doubt the Sanders camp was taking notes.

The similarities between Bloomberg and Trump—both are defined by their wealth, brashness, and New York City demeanour—make the former mayor a perfect debate proxy for the president. And no one took better advantage of this than Warren, who spent most of the debate attacking Bloomberg.

After months of Warren's restrained focus on policy solutions, many have wondered whether she could put up the fight necessary to take down Trump. Last week, she answered that question, explicitly comparing Bloomberg to Trump and tearing down Bloomberg's "history of hiding his tax returns, of harassing women, and of supporting racist policies."[40]

For the first time, voters could see just how Warren scraps. She stuck to her principles, was articulate, and proved that she can fight back without getting covered in mud.

In reality, the rumble in Nevada may not make a difference: Bloomberg's four hundred-million-dollar (USD) ad buy will reach millions more Americans than the debate did. Regardless, the catfish has been set loose in the tank.

NOT STRONG ENOUGH

To garner our attention without stoking our basest emotions, politics must be interesting without actually edging into irreverence. Here in Canada, we routinely and correctly decry the worrying sense of apathy surrounding our politics. But as the Bloomberg case reveals, controversy and drama in politics are not—in the right context—a bad thing. Indeed, the absence of intrigue in leadership races can be deeply problematic. If the eventual victor goes into a general election largely untested and unprovoked, if she never gains a whit of genuine experience on what it's like to run a gruelling campaign, to face the media not weekly but daily, then history teaches us that her chances of victory are more difficult.

No matter the political context—but especially in nomination battles— conventional ideas must be challenged, and fresh voices heard. Sadly, the propensity for risk aversion means that it is too easy for inertia to settle.

The catfish becomes a problem, though, when it turns its attention to those outside its tank.

Having a candidate in a leadership race who uses a brash, argumentative style and personal attacks to draw attention can be good, but we must be watchful and ask ourselves this question: Who do their attacks target?

Bloomberg's candidacy energized the Democratic primary. Considering that he focused on his competitors' hypocrisy and policies, I feel confident declaring that his assertive energy was a beneficial force. But when candidates target individuals or groups (particularly vulnerable groups) who exist outside the campaign environment, they can leach focus from relevant issues. Although they may succeed in drawing eyes to the campaign, overall, they take away from the legitimacy of the arguments.

Having said this, I still think that what I said in my original column and in the beginning of this commentary holds true: releasing a catfish into the tank is important. But we, as the fishermen, need to be sure the catfish remains focused on the cod.

March 15, 2020

One candidate in the race for the Conservative Party leadership
has stooped to a new low.

In CPC Leadership Race, One Candidate Stoops to a New Low

I was disappointed this week to learn that one candidate in the race for the Conservative Party of Canada leadership had stooped to a new low by besmirching the name of an opponent while hoisting the standard of racism and Islamophobia.

If you're unfamiliar with the name Jim Karahalios, you could be forgiven. After all, the Cambridge, Ontario–based troublemaker is best known for his Axe the Carbon Tax campaign and his legal disputes with the PC Party of Ontario. In other words, he is a nonentity in a race that will almost certainly come down to the two leading candidates: Erin O'Toole and Peter MacKay.

So it is perhaps unsurprising that Karahalios is relying on name-calling to draw attention to his otherwise lamentable campaign. Last weekend, Karahalios's team distributed an email attacking O'Toole and accusing O'Toole's volunteer campaign co-chair of advocating for the implementation of Sharia law in Canada.

Karahalios's decision to attack O'Toole co-chair Walied Soliman was not just desperate and inappropriate but also bizarre. For context, Soliman is a long-time party activist and fundraiser. He is widely liked and respected.

Furthermore, not only is he chair of the Canadian arm of Norton Rose Fulbright, one of the largest and most successful law firms in the world, he has served as their global chair as well.

Soliman has consistently been ranked as one of the country's top lawyers, serves on the board of Toronto's SickKids Foundation, and just months ago was recognized by the United Nations Association in Canada as its 2019 Global Citizen Laureate. His accolades speak for themselves, as does his long record of generosity and service.

But that's beside the point.

Karahalios's xenophobic attack is a reminder of the unfortunate reality that even with a reputation like Soliman's, Canadian Muslims face uniquely vicious scrutiny for their faith.

I say his record is beside the point because it simply shouldn't matter how successful or charitable an individual is. Like every other Canadian— Jewish, Christian, atheist, or otherwise—their belief (or lack thereof) should be a matter for them, their family, and their community. It most certainly should not be a political football to be lobbed in order to undercut the legitimacy of an opponent's campaign.

In a country like Canada, which prides itself on the secularism of its public sphere, we cannot lose sight of the lived experience of those who face prejudice for their faith. Even as other barometers of social progress, like the status of women and acceptance of homosexuality, have moved in the right direction, religious tolerance remains a work in progress.

It's easy to forget that just a few decades ago, some of Canada's largest cities were essentially segregated along lines of faith: Catholics lived in certain neighbourhoods, while Protestant and Jewish families lived elsewhere. While that reality has changed, attitudes toward religious diversity can still be problematic.

Think of Quebec's Bill 21, which essentially bans all religious symbols from the public sector. Not only does it send a frightening message to Muslims and other religious groups, it sows the potential for social discord.

Consider the example of a veiled woman boarding public transit. Thanks to the specifics of the law, a bus driver or transit employee is now entitled to ask her to verify her identity by removing her covering. Beyond the humiliating nature of such a request, it goes against the principle of individual liberty that a public employee should be empowered to discriminate based on someone's clothing or religious observance.

At a time when Canadians are as divided as ever along lines of geography, class, and political affiliation, it's incumbent on our leaders to face down divisive language about religion and faith, loudly and definitively condemning nonsense from the likes of Jim Karahalios.

As with the homophobic views of Richard Décarie, I look forward to Karahalios's realization that his opinions will find no home in the Conservative Party or in Canada at all, for that matter. With two weeks to go until the next leadership race qualification deadline of March 25, with a bit of luck, he will not have to wait very long to learn his lesson.

TOOTHLESS

Party brass rightfully disqualified Karahalios from the 2020 race for the Conservative Party leadership for his transgressions—vile expressions of racism and Islamophobia. But I should have explored the extent to which opinions like his appear in leadership contests and in our broader civic discourse.

Fringe candidates use leadership races to gain publicity for their radical beliefs. They are no mere benign force, especially in leadership contests for opposition parties where a radical presence can represent an existential threat. Tactically speaking, if a party has a candidate like Karahalios in its midst, it is Christmas in July for that party's opponents.

For some time, this has been especially problematic for Conservatives. But we've seen party leaders, such as Doug Ford, successfully disassociate from these characters.

The way to fix this problem is to tackle it before it starts. I'd like to propose a more robust vetting process to ensure that candidates like Karahalios never share the same stage as serious candidates. Such restrictive (and conceptually illiberal) measures may well be worth the challenges they present to ensure that bigots never acquire the sheen of legitimacy leadership contests endow.

That said, there's no dancing around the fact that any vetting process strengthened to disqualify candidates based on potentially controversial beliefs could be accused of stifling a party's ideological diversity. No matter how carefully that process is designed, there's a chance of getting it wrong and silencing the kind of vital ideas needed to widen a party's appeal.

These are valid criticisms. Convincing in theory. Less so in practice. The messy truth? A party must weigh the risk of ideological narrowness against the risk of platforming, however briefly, a harmfully prejudiced leadership contestant. Especially one who runs the risk of cementing the kind of ideological bias that plays to a stereotype the party is trying to steer away from.

Before a candidate is permitted to run, parties should ask themselves whether that individual would get fired from most mainstream Canadian businesses (or disqualified during the hiring process) for the beliefs they hold. If the answer is yes, show them the door.

September 20, 2020

With his working-class bona fides and his eye on the prize, Conservative leader Erin O'Toole may yet find a way to thread the needle and find the wide support needed to win a general election.

In a Gradual Shift to the Centre, an Opening for O'Toole

Since Erin O'Toole won the leadership of the Conservative Party and became the leader of the official opposition, the Air Force veteran and former cabinet minister has been busy waiting in line.

On Wednesday, after an hours-long delay, he and his family were turned away from an Ottawa-area testing centre. O'Toole continues to self-isolate after a potential exposure from a staffer, and he later obtained a test at a special site offering priority tests to MPs and family.

But O'Toole also wasted no time in pointing out that his experience was an indictment of the Trudeau government's failed approach to COVID-19 testing. Indeed, many testing centres are finding themselves overburdened by lengthy lineups as case numbers are on the rise and students return to school.

Many Canadians may soon find themselves in the same position as O'Toole, shivering in line at a COVID testing centre. O'Toole's latest attack may resonate with this audience, especially when combined with the imposition of new restrictions in Ontario and the second wave beginning to bear down upon us. Gone is the halo effect of competent leadership in the early days of the pandemic. Instead, we are seeing O'Toole test-driving criticisms of the government as it enters a distinctly more challenging and vulnerable phase of pandemic politics.

As his predecessor discovered, and as I wrote previously in this column, the role of opposition leader in a time of acute crisis can be difficult. They must hold the prime minister and his or her government to account, but at the same time, the rally-around-the-flag effect can insulate the government from even the mildest critique. Andrew Scheer never quite managed to find the right angle to attack Trudeau over his handling of COVID-19, because for months the prime minister cut a sympathetic figure: isolated from his wife and family, working remotely from his cottage. O'Toole's empathic approach on display with the line-waiting—"I'm suffering because of this government's mistakes, too"—may yet do the trick.

Even as he sharpens his weapons against Trudeau on the pandemic front, O'Toole's other task is to sell himself to the 905 region, and an effort to grow Conservative support beyond the base. This will require a softer approach, and a tack toward the centre that is already self-evident to those paying attention.

Take, for example, O'Toole's Labour Day greeting. "I was raised in a General Motors family. My dad worked there for over thirty years," it begins unremarkably. But by the time O'Toole is explaining to the viewer that "GDP growth alone is not the end-all, be-all of politics" and "the goal of economic policy should be more than just wealth creation—it should be solidarity, and the wellness of families," one gets the distinct sense that O'Toole's own brand of conservatism will be different from that of his predecessor.

To be specific, O'Toole seems to have his eye on union voters—GM families, as he says, just like the O'Tooles of yore. This is the same strategy used to great effect by Boris Johnson in the UK, who won his majority government in large part by breaking through the traditional, working-class "red wall" of Labour supporters. As one leftist publication concluded, "Erin O'Toole's Labour Day message should worry the Left."

Further to this goal, O'Toole has been softening some of the hard edges that Scheer neglected. He might yet march in a Pride parade, and he has been less categorical on issues such as carbon pricing—indeed, his platform promised "a national industrial regulatory and pricing regime."

Polling indicates that on both these policy matters, the party will need to align with majority opinion in the 905 if it hopes to make inroads there.

There remain some challenges to contend with, including the social conservative wing of the party, which has found a new champion in Leslyn Lewis, the breakout star of the leadership campaign. She has since found a riding, in deep-blue Haldimand-Norfolk, where she will almost certainly succeed the retiring Diane Finley.

Lewis and her like-minded supporters will expect the kind of action from O'Toole that runs contra to the party's objectives in the GTA. This is the same challenging electoral bind that vexed Scheer, but O'Toole—with his working-class bona fides and his eye on the prize—may yet find a way to thread the needle.

UNFORESEEABLE CIRCUMSTANCES

This article exemplifies the importance of political dexterity. I choose this word carefully. Politicians, by their nature, know how to twist situations to their advantage. The best of them interpret and follow the prevailing political winds. Here, the famous adage of the French politician Alexandre Auguste Ledru-Rollin applies: "There go my people. I must find out where they are going so I can lead them."[41]

Erin O'Toole exemplifies what the absence of this skill can do to a political career. When I originally wrote this article, O'Toole's movement toward the centre was not only a wise one but one I supported. In the pandemic's early stages, it seemed that the Conservative leader had positioned himself nicely as a modern-day Conservative alternative to Trudeau.

Then 2021 happened.

In a year that began with the insurrection at the US Capitol, in our own country, 2021 was characterized by a rise in the popularity of the far-right People's Party of Canada, culminating in the occupation of downtown Ottawa the following January. Pierre Poilievre and Alberta's Danielle Smith nimbly took advantage of these developments, characterizing themselves as political outsiders who had the interests of the people at heart. O'Toole, however, clung to his centrist tone, appealing to the working class not through social but fiscal conservatism. But his plan was to be for naught. The 2021 federal election, called hastily by Trudeau, came and went, along with O'Toole's chances to be the next prime minister. He was replaced by Poilievre, whose dexterity once again proved critical in his leadership race victory.

What is best learned looking back on this column is not that choosing to be centrist is a bad political decision. Instead, it's that despite obvious turning tides, O'Toole never sufficiently changed his strategy, never turned the ship around to reverse course, despite the many indications he was sailing toward the political rocks. While staying the course might feel like— and probably is—the noble thing to do, the trick to successful campaigning is altering course when necessary. Those who don't will only travel in one direction—downward.

March 27, 2022

Pierre Poilievre, Jean Charest, and Patrick Brown are all licking their chops after the announcement of the confidence-and-supply deal.

The Liberal-NDP Deal Opens a Door for Conservative Leadership Candidates

This week the prime minister simultaneously took two different risks with two very different opposition parties.

The Liberal "confidence and supply" agreement with the New Democrats was a political manoeuvre that provides stability for a minority government, while offering NDP leader Jagmeet Singh reasonable positioning as a conscientious voice in Parliament.

The price? Limiting the government's flexibility as it copes with a post-COVID world, by locking the prime minister into policies that are both popular and costly.

Notwithstanding those limitations, the decision must have been easy to make with respect to the New Democrats.

In another respect, a gamble has been taken here. The deal presents the Conservative Party with a longer runway to develop ideas and campaign tools before the next general election and provides distinct opportunities for each of the prominent leadership candidates to expand and strengthen their base. Competition to do so will be fierce; it could be the exact environment Conservatives need—if they don't tear each other apart in the process.

Pierre Poilievre, Jean Charest, and Patrick Brown are all licking their chops after the announcement.

As the loudest parliamentary voice against government excess, the deal plays well into Poilievre's pugilistic strategy. He has amassed an enviable online following and list of caucus endorsements with his harsh criticism of deficits, inflation, and incursion on personal freedoms. With this deal, Poilievre can no longer be accused of fighting a fictional bogeyman.

We know that Canadians share his concern for affordability, and many will see Liberal-NDP spending pledges as a bridge too far. When the confidence-and-supply agreement reaches its conclusion, we will no longer be in a pandemic. Our growing debt load, combined with likely increases in interest rates, will be a pain point for governments and taxpayers alike.

Who better to fight against this seemingly inevitable outcome than Canada's loudest fiscal hawk?

For the seasoned Charest, the deal presents an opportunity to prove he really is "built to win." His play will be to position himself as the Conservative best able to draw together the progressive wing, through moderate positions on climate change and social issues, as well as a credible appeal to national unity.

With the Liberals drifting away from their traditional centrist positioning—now more than just rhetorically—it stands to reason that progressive conservative voices have an opening.

Charest will have to contrast himself with other candidates, while convincing swing voters and existing party members that his team poses a credible alternative to the current government and is worth investing in.

More than that, Charest needs to convince them that it is worth taking out a membership card and joining. To do so will require not simply a compelling policy platform but also a ground organization on a scale not seen before in a partisan leadership race.

As for Patrick Brown, he has the chance to cement his base and deploy his urban organizers to attract new members. As mayor of Brampton, he has a diverse coalition of voters to serve as a springboard and a proven ability to win in a Liberal-leaning city—but with a limited profile outside of Ontario, he has considerable ground to make up.

While generally seen as a moderate, Brown did not hesitate to loudly and provocatively decry the new "socialist coalition." Campaigning against government largesse is hardly a novel strategy in Conservative leadership politics, but the newly formed Liberal-NDP alliance has added fuel to these efforts.

In fact, since the government announcement, Conservative fundraisers have found a real source of excitement and urgency. Hopefully, members will be treated to a much more aspirational debate about the role of the Conservative Party—and the role of government—in this changing political ecosystem.

By securing this agreement, Justin Trudeau has made his immediate future as prime minister much more secure, but he has also opened the door for stronger, more coherent opposition in the long-term. The playing field is open for Conservative candidates to take advantage.

Reflecting on this column as the Liberal-NDP deal unfolds has been fascinating. After emerging victorious out of a brutal CPC leadership race, Mr. Poilievre has proven that he is more than capable to handle this amalgamation of the Left, beautifully demonstrating how agreements like this can be twisted by clever opposition to reduce the popularity of both parties.

In essence, Poilievre's strategy relies on making his criticisms of Trudeau's policies something that everyone can agree with, then pointing out Singh's hypocrisy in supporting them despite these obvious drawbacks. It's a strategy he has been executing with tremendous skill.

For instance, when incidents of Chinese contact with Liberal MPs came to light, the Conservatives gained control of the narrative, arguing for a common-sense public investigation and asking questions about why the public was not notified earlier. The NDP, stuck between a rock and a hard place, supported the Conservative calls for an independent commission but did not go so far as to trigger an election.[42] This was great for Poilievre's Conservatives; they had their calls for an inquiry rationalized while simultaneously getting to call out the NDP for their hypocrisy in not calling an election.

Conservatives have also critiqued the 2023 budget, denouncing it as exorbitant in a time of high levels of inflation.[43] Their focus on the budget issue pressures the Liberals and makes it seem disingenuous for the NDP to tout the wins they were able to get into the budget. Meanwhile, the Conservatives get to market themselves as the party of the working class, again taking control of the narrative.

Consistently, Poilievre has been able to paint this alliance as an unholy one, and has positioned his Conservatives as the common-sense warriors looking to take it down.

We'll see if his opponents have inadvertently handed Pierre the tools he needs to do just that.

April 24, 2022

With every jam-packed rally, Poilievre moves that much closer to getting the keys to Stornoway and setting his sights on a bigger target.

Pierre Poilievre Has Muted "Electability" Challenges, Emerging as a Prime Minister in Waiting

I t's less than two weeks from the Conservative Party's first leadership debate, and Pierre Poilievre has established himself as the clear front-runner.

After recently dazzling over a thousand supporters at a packed Steam Whistle brewery event in downtown Toronto, the extent of his lead is such that his competitors have stopped contesting the popularity of his events.[44]

"We have been spending 100 percent of our time selling memberships," Patrick Brown's national co-chair Michelle Rempel Garner told the *Globe*.[45] Others say that Maxime Bernier also attracted large numbers without it translating proportionally to membership sales or votes.

Both counter arguments hold some truth—but it also goes without saying that any leadership aspirant would kill for the enthusiasm Poilievre has seen across the country, including in unconventional locations like, say, a downtown Toronto brewery.

The question is not whether he leads the enthusiasm race, but rather what this lead means.

Many have questioned if his online followers or rally attendees will purchase Conservative memberships and ultimately vote. That said, it is easy to believe that Canadians willing to wait in line for an hour to attend a political rally during a cold Canadian winter are as likely as anyone to show up in September. His operations team is second to none, and he will benefit from years of legwork building enduring relationships with local riding associations, campus clubs, and industry groups across the country.

Critics have also suggested that the tent he has built, while angry and vocal, is simply too narrow to be competitive in a general election. I am not so sure. I think there is a fundamental change in the attitudes of Canadians that many are missing.

While his criticism of the governing Liberals is often hyperbolic, his message to voters is a familiar one for Conservatives, characterized by smaller government, a fundamental belief in personal freedoms, and attention to pocketbook concerns.

Rather than ask whether Poilievre is too right-wing to be electable, it's a more useful exercise to examine the "third rails" that have plagued Conservative candidates in the past.

We know, for example, that the Canadian public doesn't hold the same anti-immigration sentiments as other Western nations. Our skills-based assessment process and labour-market need for more qualified workers make large-scale immigration both necessary and popular. That's why policies that appear resistant to multiculturalism, like the Harper government's "barbaric cultural practices" hotline, have unquestionably hurt the Conservatives' brand as a big-tent party.

However, Poilievre appears to understand Canadians' attitudes, rolling out a plan to speed up wait times for approving foreign credentials as an initial appeal to new Canadians and those who support their participation in the Canadian economy. Surprising many, he has also been willing to depart from social conservatives on issues like abortion and equal marriage, most recently voting with his caucus colleagues to criminalize conversion therapy.

His small-government ethos will inevitably be attacked by labour advocates as an austerity agenda, but he has been assertive and clear in contrasting his own political philosophy versus the current government's. He argues that endless dependence on printed money drives up the price of goods, only hurting Canadian workers and families.

On other issues, his path forward is less clear. While many Canadians share his criticism of the government's public health restrictions and inconsistent guidance, an even greater number watched the Ottawa convoy with horror, perplexed that any parliamentarian would stand with an illegal protest as it lay siege to our nation's capital.

God willing, the COVID-19 debate will be in the rear-view mirror by our next federal election campaign, but Poilievre must work to ensure he is not defined by his most provocative public positions.

Maintaining party enthusiasm while growing the tent has been an unmanageable balancing act for his two predecessors. But with every jam-packed rally, Pierre Poilievre moves that much closer to getting the keys to Stornoway and setting his sights on a bigger target.

THE RIGHT IDEA...

I had the right idea but had yet to fully understand how powerful the wave Poilievre was surfing was. There were Canadians willing to wait in line for an hour or more to attend a political rally during a cold winter. Canadians. Not just Conservatives. Representative clearly of the fact that Poilievre had caught a "wave."

Political waves aren't created. They're caught. And then ridden. It's often a once-in-a-generation occurrence. One that is akin to catching lightning in a bottle.

But catch it, Poilievre did. And while he learned the hard way that it did not consist of crypto-currency schemes, he did discover that mainstream pocketbook issues like government waste and the price of basic goods are very important to Canadians. Given the current economic outlook for Canada, I'm not sure it is accurate to call it a wave any longer. Pierre has connected on a deep, personal level to what everyday life is like for many Canadians.

I suggested that Poilievre would have to contend with the balancing act of retaining enthusiasm in his base while growing greater support—usually a tightrope walk for any politician. Indeed, I should have made this the leading topic of the column.

It remains to be seen (as it was when I originally wrote) whether Poilievre will successfully tread this tightrope, by growing his support while maintaining his base, just as Tony Blair did with New Labour in the UK and the way Ronald Reagan appealed to so-called Reagan Democrats, or if he'll fall into oblivion. Here's my bet: because Poilievre has actually strengthened the party's appeal by making impressive inroads with groups traditionally thought to be outside the Conservative base through coherent and persuasive "anti-elite rhetoric" aimed at union workers, immigrant communities, and young people, he'll make it across.

November 13, 2022

Those elections should not be read as a blow to populism, but as a blow to politicians who focus on the wrong priorities. This holds true across our border.

What Do US Midterms Mean for Canadian Conservatives? Not Much—The Pathetic Outing in America Was Unique to America

Tuesday's midterms turned in more than a few surprising results, with some races so close they've yet to be finalized even as I write this.[46] But one thing is clear: the widely anticipated "red wave" did not materialize.[47]

In US conservative circles, this outcome has already produced a range of impacts for the 2024 presidential race—not least being a divided GOP congressional caucus (replete with MAGA loyalists)[48] and an increasingly toxic showdown between Donald Trump and Florida governor Ron DeSantis for the party's presidential nomination.[49]

For observers here in Canada, however, the lessons for our politics amount to this: not much. What happened in America was, in my view, unique to America. It was the product of a political discourse deemed toxic by essentially everyone. It was the result of politicians caring more about themselves and the messages they wanted to drive than the concerns and the needs of the people they sought to serve.

For a country with its place of power in the world and democratic traditions, it was, to be blunt, a pathetic outing.

And that's why we have nothing to learn from what happened. It's also why the results will not impact the course charted by our Canadian political leaders and the parties they lead as they prepare for the next federal election.

In America, the set-up for the election was entirely different. Even a cursory glance at CNN or Fox News this past year would reveal that while the economy was certainly an issue, it was far from the dominant theme. Those airwaves (and virtually all others) were saturated not with talk of dollars and cents, but rather a myriad of screeching, headline-grabbing topics. Abortion rights, immigration, even the very foundation of democracy itself: the integrity of elections.

But here, things are different. Not for the truism that our people and context are different but for the reason that our opposition politicians—but in particular and most effectively, Conservative Leader Pierre Poilievre— are currently focused like lasers on the hardships Canadians are facing in their daily lives and the disappointing support they have received from their government.

It is here where Poilievre's motherlode of support is found. And let's be clear: he understands this fact. But he also understands that the growth of this support rests on continuing to make the expression of those hardships the centrepiece of his political messaging.

So this approach is not folly, as many detractors think—it is discipline. It is a series of deliberate choices. Poilievre *could* sound off on some other affair of state, but he simply will not. He is secure in the knowledge that he has found his ticket, the issue that is motivating Canadian voters. And he is right.

A lot can happen between now and 2025, when the next Canadian federal election is scheduled—a US presidential election, for one thing. But it is now a virtual certainty that today's economic pain, whether at the individual or macro level, will not abate.

But back to the midterms. Those elections cannot properly be read as a blow to populism. They can, and should, be read as a blow to politicians who focus on the wrong priorities. And this holds true across the political spectrum and across our border.

In the US, there is a relatively new term making the rounds amongst political strategists, led by its most prominent advocate, the data scientist and consultant David Shor. It's that of "popularism" and it essentially holds that, in competitive elections, message discipline is the central ingredient for success—candidates should speak almost exclusively about what's on voters' minds and shut up about what's not.

The power of this idea rests not simply in its insistence to focus solely on what polls, canvassers, and other sources of opinion confirm are the most salient issues, but also in its not-so-polite suggestion to shut up about what people *don't* care about. It's this latter insight, and the ability of the candidate and campaign to execute with flawless precision, that may be the most useful insight.

Poilievre has shown that he can convince Canadians that his priorities are the same as their own. If he can remain expressly on this path—ignoring all the friendly advice to meander or divert—and continue to stay focused on what matters to Canadians, then he will have a better-than-expected chance of winning the next election.

If the Republican Party's ineptitude has been on display since the 2022 US midterms, it has taken centre stage with its embarrassing attempt to elect a Speaker of the House in January 2023.[50] While infighting continues to escalate within the GOP, it is utterly irrelevant to us. Canada's federal Conservatives, led by Pierre Poilievre, are standing united.

My previous assertion that Poilievre effectively employed popularism (meaning: talking only about what people care about—not to be confused with popul*ism*) to avoid the stumbling blocks that flustered the GOP was accurate, but it didn't go far enough. It's not enough for the leader alone to adopt a populist strategy; the entire party must be committed to the same vision, or disaster looms.

Look no further than Kevin McCarthy, the eventual winner of that Speaker contest, as an example. He's tried to stick to his guns, pushing the narrative of Republican fiscal conservatism, but a vocal minority within the party continues to insist on a focus on that fictitious enemy—"wokeness."[51]

While this internal conflict has left the Republican Party with no coherent election campaign and their hopes in tatters, Poilievre has faced no such resistance within his own party, with former leadership opponents having either come into line or disappeared. The Poilievre Conservatives' message has been both disciplined and consistent, focusing on how Canadians are suffering due to Liberal economic mismanagement and how a Poilievre government will bring an end to the waste and reduce the cost of living.

5

—

The Trump Years

The Unwelcome Circus

Trigger warning. Reading all these columns together will remind you of what time may have allowed you to forget: the absolutely remarkable absurdity of the time, and how quickly we came to accept Trump's perversity as normalized behaviour.

Had January 6 taken a turn for the *even* worse, it's plausible that, while fearfully huddled, we Canadians might have turned to one another to remark how nice, how useful, it would have been to have seen it all coming. To have known that, as Trump descended on that escalator in the atrium of Trump Tower to announce his candidacy for president in June 2015, America's democracy was simultaneously descending into hell.

Had the unscrupulous Mike Pence cowed to his master just one last time, had his spine not magically appeared, had he refused to certify the 2020 election results, then our closest ally, one of the world's largest and most enduring democracies, might well have collapsed like the house of cards its critics have always claimed it to be.

It was actually that close.

It's difficult to say what the implications for Canada might have been. But there's no question that rampant political and civil instability in our biggest trading partner, most consequential ally, and—arguably—best friend would have been very bad news.

But very few of us saw the US Capitol attack coming.

And, regrettably, I wasn't one of the smart ones.

I'll spare you tedious self-flagellation. There's enough of that in my later columns on POTUS 45, once I had woken up to just how destructive his actions would prove to be—and, in turn, how wrong I'd been in the early years of Trump's presidency, when I told everyone to take an Ambien.[52] Near the end of his tenure, I might as well have been recommending lorazepam for the anxiety, Prozac for the panic, and morphine for the pain.

Leaving my crass prescribing practices to one side, my views on Trump—the man and his presidency—did not dramatically change over time. What did was my understanding and appreciation of the damage he had done and was doing to America's democracy and the institutions that underpin it.

Naively, I thought it would be a four-year rough patch of juvenile nonsense. I thought the elastic would snap back to its original state.

That has turned out to be profoundly wrong. A great deal of the damage Trump has caused remains raw and unaddressed. So whether he wins another election, dies tomorrow, or is thrown behind bars, his legacy will continue to shape American life for years to come.

So, what's the lesson for us here in Canada?

First and foremost, that we cannot afford to believe that America's problems can't become ours. It's especially wrong now to believe Trump's toxic approach to politics can't seep across the forty-ninth parallel. Some of it already has.

After all, there's a belief that Canada is always a few election cycles behind America in political developments and trends. For example, before our first "television" prime minister, Pierre Trudeau, they had John F. Kennedy. Before the social media campaign tactics of Justin Trudeau, the innovative 2008 Obama campaign showed the way. You can see where this might be headed.

The answer is not to enter into a paranoid state where every new Conservative politician is Trump's Canadian clone. That's a tired, sloppy argument. Trump and his circus are a singular act, and it's a show that simply does not resonate with the vast majority of Canadians. The answer is, rather, to guard against the kind of things that *do* travel: assaults on democratic institutions, scapegoating, hate speech. These are the long-term threats.

My aim in reconsidering the following columns is to deal with issues that, in hindsight, we can now clearly identify as bona fide threats to the fabric of Western democracy—or that we can instead classify as just another backfire in the engine of distraction.

In the opening chapters of his presidency, while Trump was exploding political norms left and right, making this distinction was incredibly challenging.

It no longer is. Exhibit one: tens of millions of women in the United States no longer have the right to an abortion. A Democratic president, Senate, and House were unable to undo the wrongs that led to this outcome.

I rest my case.

Typically, we've had to read between lines of speeches to gain an understanding of American policy positions. Not so with Donald Trump.

Transparent Trump Gives Ottawa an Advantage

I t was as contentious a beginning to a presidency as it was inauspicious. With the world already on edge, Donald Trump's administration spent much of its first week arguing with the media and, by extension, the public over the size of the crowd at his inauguration compared to that of the one at Barack Obama's.

In a spectacular display, Trump's press secretary Sean Spicer was sent out on Saturday to insist to a crowd of disbelieving journalists that their eyes had deceived them and that they had, in fact (or perhaps in "alt fact"), witnessed the largest crowd ever seen at an inauguration.

It was blatantly untrue. In actual fact, it was a bald-faced lie. Watching Spicer haplessly try to convince a room of experienced journalists—from the presidential press secretary's lectern, no less—of what both he and they knew to be a fabrication was as surreal as it was disorienting.

It was pure Trumpian politics.

But as we have come to expect in this Trump era, petty spectacle over optics occludes other far more significant stories. In the days since the January 20 inauguration, Trump has issued a number of executive orders that fundamentally alter long-standing positions of the US government.

A wall between Mexico and the US has been authorized. The Keystone XL Pipeline has been revived, along with the Dakota Access Pipeline.

The US has immediately withdrawn from the Trans-Pacific Partnership. Funding has been withdrawn from international groups that perform abortions or lobby to legalize or promote abortions.

And there is more. Late Friday afternoon, Trump announced that the issuing of visas to people from Iraq, Iran, Libya, Somalia, Sudan, Syria, and Yemen will be suspended for ninety days.

Each of these is a significant and abrupt policy shift from the Obama era. But none should be a surprise. After all, Trump had made it clear again and again that this is exactly what he would do as president.

Trump's actions may well be belligerent, but they are transparent as well. Transparent in way we have never seen before.

In the past, we have often been left guessing as off-the-cuff remarks from former presidents have set the world on edge. Now, we have a president who cheerfully offers every thought to open scrutiny. His tweets act like a window into his mind, a roadmap to his policies.

This presents Canada with an advantage we've not had before. Typically, we've had to read between lines of speeches, parse conversations, and spend hours analyzing congressional positions to gain an understanding of American policy positions.

In fact, the Obama administration was one of the most opaque in recent memory. Led by a man who defined himself by being measured and even-tempered, it operated in a manner that kept its opponents and allies guessing as to its true intentions.

Take, for example, the Obama administration's slow push against Israel, which developed over the course of eight years. Only in its dying weeks did the administration truly unveil how much it believed Israel to be hampering the peace process, implicitly supporting an unprecedented reprimand of Israel at the United Nations that represented a major break with historical US-Israel unity.

A second example was Obama's approach on the Keystone XL Pipeline, which provided significant challenges for the Canadian government. For close observers of the deal, it was obvious that his administration was always uncomfortable with its approval. In spite of this, Obama delayed making a decision for years out of a desire to avoid making concrete commitments.

Only in his last days in office did his administration formalize its opposition and kill the process.

Viewed through the prism of traditional government communications, Trump's administration can be seen, in one sense at least, as a breath of fresh air. His pettiness and aggressive use of Twitter offend the senses of many—for good reason, of course—but such a novel approach lends clarity for the purposes of figuring out the administration's view on any given piece of public policy.

There is rarely a question on where Trump stands on an issue. A quick scroll through his Twitter history reveals his thoughts on an entire range of topics.

As Carl Bernstein says, it provides an "MRI of his brain." It lets us understand his temperament, the way he thinks and, ultimately, his policy positions.

For the Canadian government, it is akin to playing poker with all of the cards face up on the table.

And that, regardless of what we think of the man personally, provides a never-before-seen advantage to Canada in dealing with our single most important bilateral relationship.

FUZZY
LOGIC

In the earliest days of Trump's presidency, while seemingly everyone else on the good ship Canada was sounding the alarm, crying out "SOS," and shooting off the emergency flares, here I was claiming we should not only relax but that Trump's radical new style of governing would provide us with an "edge."

Sometimes taking the contrarian stance means you're onto a truth others can't see. Sometimes it means you're the fool who remains below decks while the ship is flooding. It's safe to say that, here, the latter is a more accurate description of my opinion.

Not only was the original logic of my argument flawed, it was proven wrong by history. A history so painfully obvious that I'll stick to the logical flaws.

In my poker metaphor, our opponent had his cards face up. But what also lies on a poker table? Your chips. And gamblers know that the number of chips you possess, and how many your opponent holds, informs how you play the game. If your stack is large, you can be aggressive, even reckless. If your stack is small, you must be cautious.

A player's chips, unlike their cards, are *always* visible. Trump's stack looked like the mighty Canadian Rockies, while ours looked like, well, let's just say . . . not even the foothills. In this respect, Trump's cards scarcely mattered because his chip pile was already so high.

And yet, I was onto something. Trump's open playing style brought to light an obvious point that many Canadians had ignored for too long: that we are actually *in competition*, economically, with the US, in a contest that produces (to use two of Trump's favourite terms) a winner and a loser.

Before the Trump presidency, many Canadians happily ignored this fact. But Trump's suite of aggressively protectionist policies and the renegotiation of NAFTA brought this uncomfortable reality home.

Fierce fights have recently broken out to attract global business in the automotive, green-energy, and financial-service sectors. Better we know where we stand. How we use our smaller stack will have a deep impact on our nation's economic health.

April 30, 2017

The problem for many of the president's critics is that many Americans feel this is actually a war on them. Each attack on Trump is taken as an attack on their own values and beliefs.

Criticism Only Makes Trump More Powerful

Yesterday marked one of the first key milestones of the Donald Trump presidency: his first hundred days. It has been a turbulent introduction that has seen the new president break political orthodoxy and upend conventional wisdom.

And yet, 101 days in, the media and political establishment are no closer to understanding that they are witnessing a fundamental shift in the ground underneath them.

After spending a full year gloating about Trump's impending humiliation at the election polls, the media and Washington elite were stunned to discover that Americans had shunned their wisdom and opted for Trump.

Their initial shock has now given way to a new resistance, which has seen Congress, the judiciary, and the media each attempt, in their own ways, to foil the often ham-fisted and haphazard policy advances of the Trump White House.

Members of the establishment believe their resistance is grounded in a rousing defence of democracy, and that they are fighting out of patriotic duty. They have identified Trump's moves as borderline authoritarian and say that because he won a smaller percentage of the popular vote than Hillary Clinton, his mandate should be viewed as specious.

It isn't quite as noble a fight in the eyes of the millions of Americans who voted to install Trump as president. To them it comes across as churlish, reinforcing their belief that elitist America is willing to go to any lengths to maintain a status quo that simply isn't working for them.

In the immediate aftermath of the election, and in the shadow of Brexit, I wrote that, with the media and political establishment desperately out of touch with voters, a reckoning was needed.

Six months later, it appears that the resistance to such a reckoning has only hardened.

Every political setback Donald Trump has faced has been trumpeted as yet more evidence that he is unfit to govern. Each one has convinced the establishment that, this time, the American people have finally recognized their foolish mistake in electing him president.

His immigration directives have been blocked by the judiciary. His ramshackle, poorly thought-out health-care proposals failed to pass Congress. His administration is mocked for its incessant errors and outright lies in the media.

There have been widespread protests, social media storms, and wall-to-wall coverage of Trump's mistakes and failures.

But just what is it that this reaction demonstrates?

It demonstrates the disconnect between the reality for middle Americans and the reality for the American establishment. After all, despite the gnashing of the establishment's teeth, those Americans who voted for Trump overwhelmingly think he's doing a good job.

A recent poll found that, were the election held today, Trump would actually have defeated Clinton in the popular vote. The same poll found that of the voters who had voted Trump, only 2 percent said they regretted voting for him, with 96 percent saying that their vote for him had been "the right thing to do."

Those are hardly numbers reflective of an electorate consumed with buyer's remorse.

And yet, the tone and tenor of the coverage of President Trump has not shifted in any meaningful way. The media continues to loudly question the legitimacy of his presidency, the reasonableness of his policies, and the integrity of his character.

It's a full-on war against the president.

The problem for many of the president's critics is that many Americans feel this is actually a war on them. Each attack on Trump is taken as an attack on their own values and beliefs.

At their core, these attacks only serve to further drive Trump supporters into his sphere of influence.

By continuing to engage in this activist, anti-Trump narrative, the establishment is only empowering a president it openly despises.

Let there be no mistake: this is a president who is deeply flawed. He is inconsistent, mendacious, self-aggrandizing, and flippant. He does not appear to care about policy so much as he cares about the advancement of his own legacy.

This is a president who should be shedding support minute by minute.

But the establishment stance toward him only serves to solidify his standing among his supporters. We knew this six months ago and yet nothing has changed.

Forget Ivanka; the establishment's daily criticisms of the president may indeed be his best asset.

UNDERCOOKED

The "full on" war against Trump continued in every conceivable way and in every forum—the courts, Congress, media. Trump's supporters took this war as a personal assault on their values and beliefs. Jesus. Beer. Football. Take your pick.

It is oh-so-tempting to draw a convenient straight line from these early tumultuous days to the triumphal march on January 6 of Trump's zombie horde, those who felt most victimized by his opponents.

Let's not fail to acknowledge that if Ted Cruz had won the 2016 Republican primary (he finished in second place behind Trump) and gone on to defeat Hillary Clinton, would the Democrats really not have sought to block his legislative agenda?

Without Trump, though, the political discourse would've been less intense. That's because he was not of the old system of "elites." He didn't feel bound by their rules and approaches. He believed—likely rightly—that his base wanted the new bull to break all the china in the shop.

As a result, the war against him was more ferocious than it would have been against any of his Republican counterparts. But how could we have expected the establishment to do anything *but* wage this war? Just as Trump couldn't do anything other than be that bull, attacking orthodoxies with every tweet, the establishment couldn't help but to cling in its own way, to its own power, and to fight against him tooth and nail.

In the immediate term, the establishment's response emboldened his base of support, a cult that thrives to this day. But I was wrong in predicting that the years of negative press and obstructionist ploys wouldn't hurt Trump's popularity. It hurt him plenty. And where it was *designed* to hurt him, with swing voters. And the result of the 2020 US election speaks for itself.

Yet history proves that losers in war don't often accept defeat humbly. They embrace false narratives, find scapegoats, prepare to fight again. Today, Trump's support is more connected and organized. They share common grievances and now, a common messiah. We ought to be wary of the rematch.

January 21, 2018

Donald Trump can be credited with a number of impressive legislative accomplishments that go unrecognized thanks to all the noise and nonsense.

Don't Be Fooled by the Foolishness, Trump Is Getting Things Done

The spectacle continues.

It's fair to say that the presidency of Donald Trump looks, from the outside, to be nothing short of a circus.

The last week alone served up a heaping helping of the ridiculous. The president referred to a handful of nations as "shithole" countries, which the media gleefully plastered as headlines all over their products and platforms, right before roundly condemning the president as racist and ignorant.

Credible media outlets also obsessed over whether President Trump is six-foot-three or actually six-foot-two, and whether he could be defined as obese or not (should this now be known as the "girther" movement?).

The noise is inescapable; a frantic cycle from which we can't escape morning or night:

First, Trump makes an absurd, flippant remark. Media outlets blare headlines about the comment. The analysis from pundits frowning and condemning politicians begins. The final step: Sarah Huckabee Sanders, Trump's unshakable and inscrutable press secretary, stands in front of a room of incredulous journalists and denies that the events ever took place with a look of earnest belief.

Wash, rinse, repeat.

It is an avalanche of headlines that has begun to wear down even the most avid politicos.

These occurrences have been presented as evidence of the incompetence of the White House, or as failures of the president more generally. And, indeed, there have certainly been failures. Large and small, this White House has demonstrated that it is more than capable of getting itself into messes—time and again.

For example, the White House regularly sends news releases out with incorrect information or misspelled names. It is the sort of detail that no other White House in history would have missed—and it stands, or at least is interpreted as, an indictment of the "back office" behind the current administration.

If it can't get the little things right, how on earth can it get the big ones right?

And yet, a record is emerging. It is not the record you could have expected based on the thousands of errors, forced and unforced, that have been incurred by the White House administration in the last year.

There are actually a number of impressive legislative accomplishments; accomplishments that go unrecognized thanks to all the noise and nonsense.

For instance, a comprehensive tax reform bill that once appeared doomed due to its unpopularity recently passed the House and Senate despite the hysterical outcry of Democrats. In fact, recent polling indicates that Americans have begun to take a shine to the once-unthinkable bill, and corporations have been making high-profile announcements about returning capital and jobs to the US, crediting the changes.

Trump has also had a remarkable run in reshaping the American judiciary. While his appointment of the reliably right-wing Neil Gorsuch to the Supreme Court is certainly his highest-profile accomplishment, he has appointed a bevy of lower-ranking justices who will help to reshape and craft America's legal landscape for decades to come.

But perhaps Trump's most shocking contribution has been on the foreign-policy stage. Once derided as a know-nothing disruptor who would upset the global equilibrium, Trump's aggressive foreign policy has had significant and positive impact on the world that has received little recognition in public discussion.

His tough talk on North Korea, for instance, has been roundly mocked as unbecoming of a leader. But one of North Korea's highest-ranking diplomatic defectors went on the record to point out that North Korea looked at former presidents as considerably "gentler" than Trump, and that his rhetoric has likely spooked the regime into inaction. Indeed, it is notable that the rogue state has significantly slowed its aggressions since the war of words escalated.

Similarly, Trump's address to the United Nations criticizing the Iranian regime was derided. Pundits argued that it did nothing to unsettle the regime and had actually united Iranians behind their government. However, just a few short months later, Iran is being rocked by the strongest anti-regime protests in nearly a decade.

The declaration that Jerusalem was the capital of Israel ignited a similar furor. Allied nations and pundits were united in their condemnation that the move would cause unrest in the region.

Instead, protests in the region were relatively minor. While as expected, Saudi Arabia, Egypt, and a host of other countries condemned the move, behind the scenes, it has been reported that those countries continue to ally themselves ever closer to the United States than they had been in years past.

Daesh continues to retreat. Russia's aggressions against its neighbours have calmed. China appears wary of the unpredictable administration.

It is a foreign-policy record that many US presidents would have liked.

So, don't be fooled by the foolishness. Despite the blaring headlines and constant outrage, this presidency has made significant lunges toward its goals.

Voters are noticing. Trump's approval ratings improved last week to a seven-month high, according to poll aggregator FiveThirtyEight, though his ratings are much lower than those of other presidents at this point in their tenures.

This is not to say that the Republicans will not be shellacked in the midterms, as governing parties so often are. But it may yet be premature to write Trump's obituary as a one-term president.

CNN may just be had, yet again. The year 2020 awaits.

DEAD WRONG

Where to begin?

For a writer, or at least for me, revisiting past work is like looking at a picture of yourself. Seldom as flattering as you might've hoped for. In returning to your past ideas, you might laugh, cry, nod your head, or shake it in disgust. And if the best feeling of all is abiding pride, then the worst is stomach-churning regret. That's what I feel now.

Listen, I'm prepared to stand behind all the accomplishments I listed here. They were accomplishments any president could be proud of, and they were—at the time—overlooked. Wait. Did I say I'd classify *all* those things as achievements? Let me retract that. All of them were, except for one. And that's what was done to the judiciary. I describe Trump as having a "remarkable run" in reshaping the American judiciary, with conservative appointments from federal districts to the Supreme Court. A fact I say nothing more about.

Did I *really* not appreciate just how pernicious this "reshaping" would be?

A little over four years after I wrote this column, that Trumped-up Supreme Court would officially reverse Roe v. Wade, declaring that the constitutional right to abortion no longer existed. They generated an immediate rollback of abortion rights in nearly half the country.

Did I strike just one thing from that list of achievements? Okay, strike another. I went on to assert that Trump owned an impressive foreign-policy record. But how (even more) painfully rich that is. And here's why. Since Woodrow Wilson's Fourteen Points, US diplomatic strength has relied on a sense of exceptionalism rooted in the morality and stability of American democracy. Yet, as with all of Trump's antics, but particularly those that damaged the country's most important institutions (like the courts), it has become nearly impossible for the US State Department to scold despots whose actions it routinely condemns. "Look," they now say, "you're just like us."

Here's the bottom line. Not one of the "accomplishments" I mentioned matters one iota if the democracy and the institutions it rests upon fail.

November 11, 2018

Just weeks after the three countries declared victory, the US election results have threatened the fledgling trade agreement.

US Midterm Elections Put the Canada-United States-Mexico Agreement in Jeopardy

Another day, another bump in the road for the Canada-US relationship. Spare a moment for Minister of Foreign Affairs Chrystia Freeland. After years of arduous negotiations over a renewed North American trade agreement with a temperamental and fickle President Donald Trump, she had finally come to ground on what the government believed was an acceptable agreement.

The Canada-United States-Mexico Agreement (CUSMA) may not have won friends among certain sectors of Canada's economy but, by and large, Canadians were more than a little relieved to have escaped the renegotiation with just a few bruises and scrapes.

In the name of an assured and dependable trade relationship and the economic benefits that come with that, the country was willing to accept a deal that may not have been perfect.

But just weeks after the three countries declared victory, that fragile achievement may have been shattered.

The midterm results, delivered on Tuesday, bring with them the likelihood of disruption to American political life.

Despite the chaos that surrounds the president himself, the last two years have been relatively predictable politically due to the Republicans holding both the House of Representatives and the Senate. Pitched partisan policy battles were more or less confined to the media, rather than to the process itself.

That changed on Tuesday.

While the Republicans actually gained ground in the Senate, the House of Representatives fell to the Democrats.

The result? Nancy Pelosi is likely to assume the Speaker's chair. Pelosi is a particularly formidable partisan foe; indeed, she is one of the few Democrats whose steely approach and steady nerves have won her Trump's respect.

But even if the Speaker's gavel goes to someone else, the flipping of the House will cause major headaches for the president—and by extension, to his legacy projects, including CUSMA.

The Democrats feel they have been given a mandate to fight the president tooth and nail on his agenda. They are diametrically opposed to his ideas almost across the board and have publicly indicated their intention to do everything they can to prevent the implementation of his agenda.

However, one of the only places the president and the Democrats seem to find some common ground is around their suspicion of free-trade agreements.

The Democrats have long eyed such agreements warily, seeing them as a way to undermine sovereignty, empower corporations, and surreptitiously attack workers' rights. While that wariness faded somewhat during the mid-90s, it has not dissipated entirely. And it is a particular hobby horse of the left-wing of the Democratic Party, which finds itself in the ascendancy after this week's results.

Add to that the fact it is no secret to anyone that Trump thinks little of the North American trading relationships as they currently stand.

This means that in an environment where the House of Representatives and the president strongly disagree on virtually every issue, trade agreements may be the one area of agreement that can be used to advance other agenda items.

Indeed, the presumptive chair of the House Committee on Ways and Means, Richard Neal, has publicly pooh-poohed CUSMA. He has suggested that in order to garner the support of Democrats (a necessity for the agreement to come into force) there would need to be several additional assurances and he has also implied it may require changes.

Enter a pained Minister Freeland.

It will be up to the minister, who has spent months trekking back and forth to Washington coaxing the president's team into the deal, to now sell the deal to an equally skeptical audience for wholly different reasons.

The chances that CUSMA becomes a casualty of domestic policies are high—so Minister Freeland will need to work quickly to build a coalition of moderate Democrats and Republicans in the House who would be willing to advance the agreement quickly.

The minister, and her team, have been proven capable of doing that many times before—but it will take another level of adeptness to usher through a controversial deal in an environment as fraught and raucous as this.

But, just as before, her government's fate depends on their success—and a collapse of the agreement just months before a federal election would almost certainly be a harbinger of more negative news to come.

EGG ON MY FACE

And yet, the Canada-United States-Mexico Agreement (CUSMA) came to be after all—replacing NAFTA. What looked like a project that was destined to fail instead turned into a last-minute success story, helping to restore relations between Canada and the US that seemed rocky at best during negotiations. CUSMA, which remains largely unchanged from NAFTA, stabilized Canada-US relations and re-energized trade between the two nations.

This piece portrays the importance of a strong, clever, and motivated team in intense political negotiations. I highly doubt that Trudeau or Trump would have been able to get this deal signed without the aid of their teams. For instance, the US ambassador to Canada, Kelly Craft, as well as Blackstone Group CEO Stephen A. Schwarzman were key individuals for the US during the negotiations, settling discussions and gaining concessions that allowed the deal to go forward. Freeland herself should not be ignored: her calculated political moves no doubt helped secure the elevated status in Trudeau's cabinet she holds today.

This is a teachable moment.

In politics, leaders tend to surround themselves with like-minded people, often because, while getting things done, it can seem to them as though the whole world is against them.

That instinct is half-wrong. You need to surround yourself with those who, while sharing your core beliefs, provide a true 360-degree perspective.

With this in mind, it becomes obvious why Trump's administration was a dumpster-fire failure. Famously, his central team was a revolving door of scam artists and family friends, all of whom would rather have died than question Trump's "genius." While Trump was an extreme example of this behaviour, he is hardly unique. Those who cannot accept criticism are destined to fail in political life. Because if they don't get it from their team, they will run into a buzz saw in the real world.

December 9, 2018

Once considered a patrician, the pundits crowed about the one-term president's gentle nature and impeccable manners. Instead of calling attention to his bumbling on policy, experts wrote of his pragmatism and cautiousness in a world that was teetering on chaos.

Presidential Successors Put Bush Sr. in a New Light

Many believe that, in politics, your successor is your legacy. Consider the straight-as-an-arrow Sunday-school teacher Jimmy Carter after the Machiavellian Nixon years.

Or the steady, competent, experienced John Tory after the roller-coaster term of Rob Ford.

Or more recently, Doug Ford's approach to smaller government focused resolutely on everyday family affordability after more than a decade of big, bold Liberal schemes.

But the state funeral of the forty-first president of the United States, George Herbert Walker Bush, earlier this week also reminded us that a politician's successors can also create new frames, and new prisms, with which to view their predecessor.

As every living president, along with not just the entire American political establishment but leaders from around the world—even Charles, the future King of England was there—jammed into the magnificent Washington National Cathedral there was an elephant jammed in with them.

And it wasn't the elephant that serves as the GOP's mascot and logo.

Rather, it was the astonishing divide between the forty-first president and the forty-fifth, President Donald Trump.

As our own former prime minister Brian Mulroney opened his tribute, Trump could be seen slumping in his pew, his arms aggressively crossed on his chest, and a surl on his lips. But he was alone.

The rest of the congregation was right with Mulroney as he offered, "I believe it will be said no occupant of the Oval Office was more courageous, more principled, and more honourable than George Herbert Walker Bush."

Mulroney went on to provide a *tour de table* of Bush's accomplishments: the Gulf War, NAFTA, the Clean Air Act, leadership that was "distinguished, resolute, and brave."

Others went on to describe the forty-first president as the last of the "soldier statesmen," as one of the last of the "greatest generation."

And with each accolade, with each remembrance, the difference between George H. W. Bush's leadership and that of the current occupant of 1600 Pennsylvania Avenue became more painfully acute.

The sense of loss of decency in public life became clearer.

And with that how both Americans and the world thought about their former president began to change.

After all, despite all his successes, which were recounted this week, Bush lost the presidency in 1992, after just one term.

A young upstart named Bill Clinton seemed more in tune with the times. He reflected the optimism and freshness that was felt across the country. President Bush, on the other hand, while familiar and reliable—not unlike a panelled station wagon that had served dutifully—was more like yesterday's news.

But Bush only knew one way to be president and he stood by it. He allowed journalists, historians, and pundits to see him as a bumbling patrician.

Incredibly, the *New York Times* story that came to define his presidency reported Bush had been dumbfounded by a grocery store barcode scanner and didn't know the price of a quart of milk.

The story, and its implication that he was woefully out of touch, had the ring of truth, and defined Bush for a generation.

But that sentiment dissipated significantly this week, as experts reflected on Bush's presidency in the wake of his passing.

Rather than call him a patrician, the pundits crowed about his gentle nature and impeccable manners. Instead of calling attention to his bumbling on policy, experts wrote of his pragmatism and cautiousness in a world that was teetering on chaos.

Some went so far as to say he was the best one-term president since James K. Polk, who served in the nineteenth century.

Today, Bush's legacy stands in marked contrast with the one predicted in 1993, after his re-election loss.

By comparison, President Clinton, who had long enjoyed the highest approval ratings in the country, has suffered from historical consideration. His personal behaviour has clouded his policy successes and his approval ratings have dropped significantly.

It turns out how you lead, like how you live your life, actually matters. That what Saint Francis taught is right: in consoling we are consoled, in giving we receive, and in pardoning we are pardoned.

And that's why I don't think it is random that the Bush family motto is, "*Et ius illud*," which when translated to English means, "Do the right thing."

CLOSE BUT NO CIGAR

How will Donald Trump be remembered in decades to come? Likely in just as polarizing a light as he is today.

Why?

Apart from giving Barnum & Bailey a run for their money, Trump's presidency was utterly unremarkable. And so, his acolytes will be left clinging as much to the myth that was Donald Trump as to anything that he actually achieved. (That's not to say his presidency was inconsequential. Given Trump's malevolent appointments to the judiciary, America will have to live with the hangover from his presidency for at least a generation).

So, how did I do? I think I was correct in my idea of why history has been good to Bush Sr. and why Trump will experience the reverse.

It's my view that Trump's popularity does not signal a fundamental or structural change in the firmament of American public opinion, but rather a reactionary one to a set of circumstances that are unlikely to endure.

When Trump came to power, many in America were hurting. Feeling left out. Left behind. Tired of being talked at instead of listened to. Trump was a powerful antidote to all of that.

But I just don't believe that all the previously held sacred norms will be discarded that easily. And I refuse to believe Trump's damage to the most significant of those sacred norms—the primacy of truth-telling in politics—is a legacy that will outlive the man.

I do believe that the things Bush Sr. stood for are more firmly set into the American psyche and will matter more, not less, with the passage of time.

Here's where I got it wrong, though. In my rush to tear down one specious myth, I elevated another. An uncritical myth of Bush Sr. is a problem itself. I should have known better.

June 21, 2020

When I see Americans pitted against each other in an overdue demand for justice for African Americans, I no longer have to hypothesize about what happens when a leader governs for some of the people and not all of the people.

As America Cries for Leadership, Donald Trump Accelerates Its Division

Ever since that poignant morning in 2016 when Hillary Clinton took the stage in bipartisan, conciliatory purple to concede defeat to Donald Trump, I have used this space to urge people to remain calm. To remind them that America is a mature and stable democracy that will cope just fine with the tumult of a Trump presidency.

I have written that the markets will continue to function, Congress will do its job, the courts will defend the Constitution and the military will refute any unlawful order.

Far from a Trump apologist, I was anchored in a belief that the breadth of modern America's institutions—legal, civil, and economic—can be depended upon to not only withstand but to keep in check the most dangerous impulses of any character who ascends to the Oval Office.

It is now clear I was mistaken.

Like a lot of people, I think, I allowed the good times or at least "normal" times of the day colour my lenses in imagining the impact a disastrous president could have. I never considered what would happen in bad times and how devastatingly wrong that analysis would turn out to be.

Now five months into a pandemic that has brought with it uncontemplated social and economic disruption, I no longer have to hypothesize about the theoretical impact of an unhinged presidency.

When I see Americans pitted against each other in an overdue demand for justice for African Americans, I no longer have to hypothesize about what happens when a leader governs for some of the people and not all of the people.

I can simply watch the catastrophic results play out in front of my eyes every night on Fox or CNN.

To be sure, three years of President Trump has been a revolving door of disaster. The juvenile insults, assaults on civil rights, violent outbursts, and episodes of corruption have flowed from one to the next.

But now that the "good times" or the "normal times" are well and truly over and our world has been jolted from normalcy, we can clearly see the price America is paying for his nonsense.

At a time when America is being rocked to its very core, when Americans are yearning, no, crying out, for a steady hand, for a North Star, for hope, there is none to be found on Pennsylvania Avenue.

Clearly, Americans have endured bad presidents before. Just as we in Canada have had bad prime ministers. But it is hard to remember a time when a leader has so emphatically disengaged with their role as a leader in a time of crisis. It is even harder to imagine another White House responding to nationwide hurt and anguish with such a leering sense of menace.

When it comes it its government, America has much of which to be proud. In modern times it survived, for example, the disgrace of Watergate. By its example, it has contributed to democracy around the world. It has made its own way in that world and created a presidency that fulfills the role of not only the head of government but also the head of state. A leader comparable to the political role of a prime minister who is also endowed with the monarch-like responsibility to model a nation's leadership and help absorb its pain.

Within that construct, there are some things that others can do, some that only the president can do.

For example, the president is often referred to as the comforter-in-chief. It is a role that Presidents Reagan, Clinton, and Obama fulfilled to great effect. But the truth is, it is a responsibility that can be delegated to another leader. The vice-president or a religious leader for example.

But what can't be delegated is the role the president plays when the nation needs to come together. When differences need to be set aside and common ground found. In those times, there is no substitute for the president.

The problem American faces today is Trump, by his own actions and his own hand, has forfeited that role.

By the Constitution, he retains his legal authority to govern. But by pitting one American against another, he has lost his moral authority to lead.

BANG ON

My closing statement that Trump lost the moral authority to lead the American people raises an important question: So what?

Implicit in my claim that a leader without moral authority sows division is the idea that division is cancerous, that it will—eventually—give rise to civil war, the fall of Rome, total anarchy, the end of time.

But is the absence of moral authority, specifically from a country's leader, *really* so potentially catastrophic, or is there something deeper at play?

In many respects, we've come a long way from what many might consider to be quintessential examples of presidential moral authority. Roosevelt after Pearl Harbour. Kennedy after the Cuban Missile Crisis. Bush Jr. after 9/11. Revealingly, Republicans and Democrats violently disagreed with these presidents' decisions regarding such perilous events. And yet, these leaders were able to effectively put partisanship on hold to direct the American people to face a larger existential struggle.

Today, in many ways, things are still the same. In times of crisis, leaders need moral authority. And that explains why the absence of it under Trump during the COVID-19 pandemic was so troublesome.

Of course, if Hillary Clinton had been in office at the outset of the pandemic, she would have faced her own challenges. I can picture it now: a torrent of conspiracy theories that the pandemic was a hoax engineered by the Clinton administration. But I think she would have done better. It's a fair bet that she wouldn't have torched the bully pulpit of the presidency, like Trump did, and therefore that she would have been able to use moral suasion to greater effect.

For this reason, I think America would have come through the crisis in markedly better shape.

So, my answer is this. The bully pulpit that is the American presidency is at its most powerful when it is occupied by a leader with moral authority.

May 9, 2021

Many expected that any president who followed one as disruptive as Trump would need to be a transitional president. One who would give the country time to catch its breath and to throw off the chaos of the previous four years. Instead, Biden is moving by leaps and bounds to transform the role of the state in American life.

Biden Has Taken Up the Challenge of His Office and Its History, Proving Trump's Impact to Be Impermanent After All

For those on Twitter or otherwise tuned into the political world's 24-hour spin cycle, the past hundred days have been marked by an unusual phenomenon: the casual hum of political discourse in the absence of Donald J. Trump.

On the streets and in the news, Trump's legacy marches on through COVID denial, hysteria about the "BIG LIE" of election fraud, and the steady purging from the Republican Party of common sense and dissenting opinions.

But the troller-in-chief himself has been notably absent from the airwaves, providing nary a peep on social media. He's barely engaging in interviews, or even appearing in public for that matter.

Of course, Trump's quiet is due in part to his exile from the platforms he once held dear, but it is also a sign that his grip on American life is fading—that most Americans have tuned out his vision of the world.

Astonishingly, it may turn out that after all the insanity of the last four years, the damage and the impact of Trump may prove to have been all sound and fury. That the impact may be as ephemeral as the man is bellicose. With a legacy as enduring as a Popsicle in the summer sun, save for the wretched cultural division it has created.

For the past four years, many people—myself among them—have despaired at the damage Trump inflicted on the stature and legacy of the American presidency. He eschewed norms, abandoned allies, and at times transformed the pageantry of the office into a pantomime or worse, an infomercial.

"How," I wondered, "will his successor ever achieve any measure of greatness with an office so diminished in stature both in the nation and the world?"

For that reason, many expected that any president who followed one as disruptive as President Trump would need to be a transitional president. One who would give the country time to catch its breath and to throw off the chaos of the previous four years.

After the Watergate scandal, for example, left the presidency in tatters, it took the presidencies of both Ford and Carter before Americans were ready for another transformative president—Ronald Reagan.

Now, just over one hundred days since Trump left office, President Biden is determined to avoid the same fate. Far from proving Trump's erosion of the office irreparable, Biden has shown himself capable of being so much more than simply an interim president.

In fact, he has chosen the opposite playbook. Biden has surprised many by enthusiastically and unapologetically taking up the mantle of his party. He has paid homage to its history by expanding the American social safety net in ways unprecedented since the mid-twentieth century. With a sure-footedness that belies his status as a rookie president, Biden is moving, leaps and bounds, to transform the role of the state in American life. If he succeeds, his legacy will be paralleled only by Franklin D. Roosevelt and Lyndon B. Johnson.

What's more, Biden's undertaking is about much more than an injection of spending or increased supports for the middle and working classes. It is a move to reshape the social contract Americans have with one another and their government. And in doing so restore the stature—and power—of the presidency itself.

In his speech to both houses of Congress last month, Biden spoke of his plans as a "once-in-a-generation investment in our families and our children," acknowledging the position of his undertaking alongside FDR's New Deal and LBJ's Great Society. Whatever moniker is bestowed on his own administration's legacy—even if there is none at all—no one can call it an interim presidency.

If he fails to pass the legislation foundational to his vision, Biden will nonetheless have proven that the president *can* attempt truly transformational change. That the office he holds can still live up to the challenge of its history. In doing so, Biden will help to clear the rubble of his predecessor, further drowning out the sound and fury of a past presidency that stood for little beyond its own grim world view.

OOPSIE DAISY

Wow, this feels like I was caught up in the high of a normal presidency. After years of Trump drivel, the prospect of a motivated and seemingly well-meaning president stunned me as to the reality of the situation in the United States.

To be fair to my past self, my argument that the presidency miraculously survived the Trump era is still largely accurate: the institution remains a key international force. Much of the damage Trump inflicted attached to him and, mercifully, not the institution. Biden governs as though there never was a Trump and keeps pushing out bold legislation targeted at supporting his middle- and working-class voter base. But while the presidency may have survived relatively unscathed, the political structure surrounding it has fallen into disrepair.

Take, for instance, the state of the Republican Party. What used to be a party of fiscally conservative opposition has mutated into a hate-filled and corrupt version of itself, fighting the invisible demons of the "woke mob"[53] and the "deep state."[54] This evolution has seriously damaged the fabric of American society, whose two-party democratic system is under serious threat of collapse. Look no further than the policies implemented by Republican governors attacking LGBTQ2S+ and women's rights, freedom of the press, and education systems. There are now Republican state legislatures asking to secede from the union, which merely ten years ago would have been considered unfathomable.[55]

This rise in hatred certainly did not start with Trump. But he is undoubtedly to blame for its rapid ascendancy, both in the US and abroad. His hold on American conservatives is airtight, and if I'm right about Trump's personality, he won't be letting go anytime soon. Worst-case scenario, prudent American conservatives are gone for good, having been replaced with this lunacy permanently. Hopefully I'm wrong.

June 20, 2021

The leaders at last week's G7 summit in Cornwall seemed content to pretend the last four years of contentious feuding and embarrassing breaches of protocol had been a blip. But the fault lines that delivered Donald Trump to office are still very much active.

World Leaders Seem to Think the Trump Years Were Nothing But a Bad Dream. It's Time for Them to Wake Up

L ast week's G7 summit in Cornwall was the very model of modern, multilateral politicking. Against the backdrop of sunny beaches and clear blue skies, leaders of some of the world's largest economies walked and talked, posing together every step of the way.

Pre-summit hopes had been in overdrive. Cornwall was, after all, the first such summit in the so-called post-COVID era, and the first G7 attended by the new leaders of Italy, Japan, the United States, and the European Union. A more civilized, internationalist approach to the issues of the day seemed to be heralded by the inclusion of leaders from Australia, India, South Korea, and South Africa.

But despite all the promise of a brighter tomorrow inherent in the summit, a crippling sense of nostalgia or, more accurately, amnesia turned out to be the dominant theme.

Perhaps that's because, to a person, the leaders onstage seemed content to pretend the last four years of contentious feuding, silly gamesmanship and embarrassing breaches of protocol and convention had been a blip. A speed bump on the otherwise open road to greater co-operation and interdependence among nations.

Indeed, apart from elbow bumping in lieu of handshakes, the summit could well have taken place in 2015—before COVID wrought havoc over the globe, before Donald Trump walked all over the idea of unity among Western allies with his grandstanding.

But no amount of self-congratulatory affection between Western leaders could return us to that halcyon era. So, we were instead forced to watch as the G7 proved itself unable to grapple with reality. In the process, it became painfully obvious that the institution is not fit for purpose.

Sure, some accomplishments were achieved—but they entailed a healthy dose of hypocrisy.

The meeting agreed to donate one billion COVID vaccines to the COVAX sharing initiative—though Canada's own contributions will only come from returning the vaccines it took from COVAX in the first place!

The gathered countries also pledged to support the education of forty million girls globally. Sadly, this pledge has been described as an "empty promise,"[56] given the host country's own decision to cut its overseas aid commitments—including those aimed at girls' education!

Although leaders reached an agreement on reducing carbon emissions, ultimately it is woefully insufficient in the eyes of climate advocates. Activist Greta Thunberg sarcastically noted that "G7 leaders seem to be having a good time presenting their empty climate commitments."

But perhaps the greatest oversight of all was on the part of world leaders who celebrated the return of a US president who is "part of the club," to quote French president Emmanuel Macron.

The unfortunate reality seems to be that Macron, German chancellor Angela Merkel, and their fellow internationalists—our prime minister included—are behaving as though the Trump years were an aberration, rather than a sign of the times. They forget that a plurality of Americans and a majority of Republicans have made it clear they'd rather blow up their club altogether.

Of course, a large part of this complex stems from the group's disdain for Trump. Aside from Britain's Boris Johnson, no G7 leader could stand the former president. Because they found him so repugnant, they refused to acknowledge his legitimacy or his impact on the global order. And they refuse to imagine that the US may well return to his form of politics.

But given the state of the American public opinion, it is not inconceivable that a more palatable Trump minion could be sworn into the Oval Office in 2025.

And there is one leader who is wise to this possibility: Russian president Vladimir Putin. Following their meeting, Putin capitalized on political rifts in the US by questioning the legitimacy of arresting those involved in the January 6 uprising.

"People came to the US Congress with political demands . . . they're being called domestic terrorists," Putin said.

For his part, Putin clearly understands the same fault lines that delivered Donald Trump to office are still very much active. Let's hope his Western counterparts wake up to the same.

HOME RUN

Well, it certainly seems that the G7 leaders slept through their alarms.

The right-wing groundswell ignored by the leaders of the free world manifested into serious electoral challenges in most G7 countries. Be it the "Freedom Convoy" here at home, Macron's narrow victory over Marine Le Pen in France, or the victory of the far-right Brothers of Italy Party, Trump's election, in retrospect, was a sign that the time of ideological progress and co-operation had ground to a halt.

But if you look closer, this global descent into a far-right embrace is symptomatic of a larger reality. During the Trump presidency, most of the G7 either didn't see or chose to ignore just how influential US culture and politics still are on the international stage.

"But Jaime," I hear you protesting, "nobody doubted that the US is powerful, even when Trump was in control!" Perhaps, but it certainly seemed like G7 leaders were determined to wait for cooler heads to prevail, ignore the US, and carry on as usual while Trump was present.

Meanwhile, the worldwide appeal and influence of US-centric news meant that conservative parties and citizens were affected globally. "If they're so successful, why don't we do that?" called the right-wing parties of the West.

Other factors (an increased migrant presence and economic stress) have rocked liberal governments across Europe. But there can be no questioning that Trump's victory had a serious impact on right-wing parties and electorates across the world: Nordic states' left-wing exit and new far-right foothold,[57] [58] the revolving door of leadership for Britain's Conservatives, and the rise in popularity of the People's Party of Canada. It's the US right-wing's world, we're just living in it.

The largest consequence of this liberal fumble has been Russia's (and, to a lesser extent, China's) reaction. Putin utilized this historic uncertainty in democracy to launch his war in Ukraine while attempting to undermine the US-led global order. While for the moment Western states have rallied against this open threat, time will tell whether these stricken Western institutions can hold up against the battering winds of Russian aggression.

6

———

The COVID-19 Crisis

Writing Through Crisis

Let's not mince words.

When it comes to the opinions we wish we'd never held, we all do our best to hide them away. We try to forget that our beliefs were ever so misguided in the first place. And to be sure those ideas stay buried, especially those most contentious, we let others do the same.

Needless to say, a global pandemic that has killed more than seven million people falls squarely into this category.[59]

After all, no one wants to be on the wrong side of history—particularly in the digital age, when all it takes is a quick search to resuscitate damning disclosures, and a simple click of the "post" button to share the receipts.

Most people, therefore, walk away from those opinions and beliefs proven by time to have landed on that mistaken side. But the whole idea behind this book is to do the exact opposite: to restore them from the deleted folder and to face them head-on.

Why?

Because hindsight, particularly concerning the most contentious of issues, is what instructs, provides genuine insight and understanding, and, most crucially, guidance for the road ahead—a road on which we are almost certain to encounter similar issues, problems, and challenges yet again.

Concerning the COVID-19 pandemic, we're not talking about the simple opinions of daily life—Pepsi versus Coke, Beyoncé versus Rihanna, the Habs or the Leafs. Rather, we're talking about opinions that either saved or jeopardized lives and livelihoods. That tore not just families but significant portions of our society apart.

The challenge, of course, was that there was no time to get it right. There was always a certain sense of distress combined with the dread of uncertainty. And it wasn't as if there was anyone out there with better data, with the complete picture—someone who knew exactly what to do. No such person or data set existed.

When the full and final history of this pandemic is written, if ever it is, we won't be able to overlook the fact that it unfolded in a new age of information, where a deluge of innovative ideas, absurd conspiracies, false narratives, and shrewd insights all not only collided but competed.

Accordingly, nowhere in this book is the chronological arrangement of columns so significant, because—in this more condensed period—these columns provide a study on the evolution of opinion in the crunch time of crisis. More than just "history on the run," writing columns during a crisis amounted to scribbling in a full sprint, while the information landscape underneath my feet was constantly giving way.

For many Canadians, it felt, as it did for me, that we had run this race before.

I was a very close adviser to the Ontario government in 2003 during the SARS outbreak in Toronto. Back then, we learned very painful lessons. Consequently, I was confident we would be better prepared for future health crises than other countries, and in many significant ways, we were.

But our high horse was not tall enough to keep us out of the mire.

As painful and unhelpful as it is true, we all struggle to learn from our mistakes. I often think there are two major barriers that prevent us from doing so.

The first arises from failing to *face* the error. After an arduous experience, we may desire overwhelmingly to move on. So, step one: confront the facts.

The second barrier occurs when we try to take that first step too quickly, too carelessly. We may see the world divided into heroes and villains to celebrate or scapegoat. We may fall victim to digestible platitudes and miss important nuances in between.

The beauty of returning to columns written during the era of COVID-19 is that doing so helps circumvent both barriers. In the following columns and commentaries, I'll testify that miscalculations were made, and that we can learn from our errors. Moreover, I'll attempt to go beyond extremes or simplified narratives.

In doing so, I will take that vital first step. I'll face the reality of what I had to say, what I got right, and what I got wrong, before I move on.

After all, while we can't know when, we all know more pandemics are on their way.

March 8, 2020

Over the past thirty years, there has been an observable decline in our collective confidence in institutions like government, "big business," news media, and democracy at large.

The Spread of COVID-19 Has Revealed an Epidemic of Mistrust

A s the latest coronavirus outbreaks have reached us at home, Canadians' concern has morphed into a growing hysteria. The virus will, no doubt, have some long and lingering effects on our economy and tragic consequences for some of our elderly and most vulnerable populations.

But in the grand scheme of things, the panic is unwarranted. While every Canadian should be careful to protect themselves and their families, the end of times this is not. COVID-19, like the other coronaviruses that came before it, will pass.

Here in Ontario, we are arguably more prepared than ever, thanks to the experience of the 2003 SARS outbreak. Our ministries of health—federal and provincial—have learned tough lessons from that episode, particularly regarding the breakdowns in communication that marred an effective response.

What's more, thankfully, we in Canada also have the benefit of governments at every level who understand that a health crisis should be managed by scientists and experts, not politicians.

That said, while we can be confident in our governments' response, the COVID-19 issue has revealed a larger problem: the epidemic of mistrust Canadians have in their public institutions. Over the past thirty years, there has been an observable decline in our collective confidence in institutions like government, "big business," news media, and democracy at large.

This trend is not unique to Canada, but rather a problem throughout the developed world. Thirty years ago, 41 percent of Americans trusted their federal government "always or most of the time." Last year, the same pollster found that number had dropped to 17 percent. For specific institutions, the numbers are not much better. Over three decades, Americans' confidence in the presidency and Congress declined 34 percent and 21 percent, respectively.

Brexit, Donald Trump, and other manifestations of populism are all results of this decline. And even in otherwise healthy democracies, this deficit of trust has damning implications in times of crisis; no better evidence of which is the ongoing reaction to the spread of COVID-19.

From the moment China alerted the WHO to cases of an unusual respiratory virus in the Wuhan region, suspicions abounded. After so many lies and half-truths to the world about even the smallest things, the Chinese government has made it impossible for anyone to trust them. So, when Beijing deployed a stream of apparatchiks to assure us that everything possible was being done to contain the virus, skepticism was the default response.

Iran, the country with the highest reported coronavirus death rate, has stubbornly refused to share information and delayed crucial action to manage the outbreak. What's worse, recent events like the downing of Ukrainian International Airlines Flight 752 have eradicated Iranians' trust in their leadership, and in turn their willingness to listen to the advice of health agencies and ministries.

In the West, our response to the crisis has been hampered by mistrust, as well. President Trump has done his best to "own" the crisis, appointing Mike Pence as the White House's coronavirus czar and making an appearance in the press-briefing room, which has been dormant since July.

But for all his best intentions—questionable as they are—the president's actions have only served to stoke distrust and paranoia. On Wednesday night, Trump went so far as to suggest that the virus is a Democrat "hoax," cooked up to hurt his chances for re-election. What does it say when the US president questions the authenticity of an epidemic that has already claimed the lives of twelve of his fellow citizens?

In times like these, the rot of skepticism and mistrust can prove fatal.

Reading the National Advisory Committee's report on SARS and public health, I was struck by the language that riddles the section on "systemic deficiencies" in Canada's response.

Chief among these deficiencies were the absence of protocols, uncertainties about data ownership, inadequate capacity for investigation, lack of coordination, and weak links between health stakeholders. Each of these factors is marked by a failure of communication and exacerbated by a culture of mistrust, delegitimized institutions, and general paranoia.

How frightening then that such is the time in which we are living; when we most need to trust, we find that we just can't.

WHERE'S MY RED PEN?

I want to focus on one statement I made early in this column, that Canadians "have the benefit of governments . . . who understand that a health crisis should be managed by scientists and experts, not politicians."

On the naivety scale, I'd rank this one pretty high. My declaration oversimplified the COVID-19 crisis as a distinctly scientific problem. I failed to appreciate just how complex this kind of issue can become when the ability of scientists, in this case, public health officials, is called into question.

A government's ability to manage *any* crisis is an inherently political issue. Political games will be played—particularly if things go south. With infections spiking and hospitals flooded, many in the scientific community blamed government leaders for not taking more extreme lockdown measures. By the same token, government leaders accused members of the scientific community for failing to grasp the full implications of lockdowns, including the mental and financial damage they did to people's well-being. And round it all went.

Covering this ground would've allowed me to explore the epidemic of mistrust in public institutions at a deeper level and make more explicit, compelling predictions.

As I remind my readers, trust was already declining *before* COVID-19 took hold. Matters worsened when, throughout the pandemic, we saw institutional figures, in the form of public health officials, doctors, and politicians, duking it out over which course of action was correct. Debate isn't an explicitly unhealthy thing for democratic society. But, given the high stakes and fraught timing, it did zero favours for people's dwindling trust in institutions.

I see now that I wrote this column thinking of an imaginary world in which science provides straightforward answers that all people can readily adopt and understand, where, if only feckless leaders got out of the way, the world of politics would not saturate everything. Perhaps it isn't that politics should leave the table but that these institutions should share it and mutually devise a coherent message. Public trust would be much easier to win if it were obvious our institutions trusted each other.

If only life were that easy.

April 12, 2020

What every strongman has understood, from Cecil to Orbán, is that a frightened public is also a compliant public. For the sake of our democracy, our leaders must understand that while we are willing to be compliant, to do our duty, to surrender some of our individual rights and liberties for the collective good, we are not frightened.

Democracy in the Time of COVID-19

Among the more concerning broader societal consequences of the coronavirus—economic collapse, fear-mongering, widespread distrust—is a stunningly rapid deterioration of democracy.

To exploit popular anxiety as a pretence to seize power is a tactic as old as plague itself. When William Cecil, chief minister to Queen Elizabeth I, was battling the plague, he won the ability to shut the sick inside their homes for up to six weeks (likely reasonable enough). But then James I went on to pass the Plague Act of 1604, which banned any criticism of this unprecedented power.

Dealing effectively with pandemics can reasonably support the suspension of some norms and freedoms, but a careful balance must be struck.

We have already seen the virus extinguish popular protest movements from Iran to Hong Kong. Now, in some places, we are seeing how it threatens democracy itself.

To be clear, this is not about the lockdowns, quarantines, and mandatory physical-distancing measures imposed by almost every responsible government in response to COVID-19. But even these sensible rules, in most cases guided by the advice of public health authorities, have resulted in penalties that can be unduly heavy-handed. Steep fines, such as the three-hundred-thousand-dollar one levelled against a Brampton-area man who hosted a backyard party for twenty friends, are an example. Surely there are reasonable limits to such sanctions.

What does concern me are the ominous cases of democratic rollbacks, like the ones we are now witnessing in Hungary. Earlier this month, Prime Minister Viktor Orbán pushed through a draconian law that allows the prime minister to rule by decree, suspend Parliament, and repeal any existing law and do so indefinitely.

The state will now impose years-long jail terms for sharing nebulously defined "fake news," or acting to impede the response to the virus, giving the authorities wide latitude to imprison political dissidents. While these measures firmly tip the EU member state from democracy to dictatorship, the rest of the Union, mired as they are in their own COVID-19 response problems, hardly seem to have noticed.

Hungary is not walking this dangerous path alone. In Thailand, the prime minister has used his new powers to impose harsh curfews and expand censorship of the news media. In Chile, the military patrol the streets and public squares, having conveniently crushed protestors who had disrupted the country for months before the virus arrived.

And the list goes on. Amid the panic of the pandemic, it can be difficult to detect where, exactly, the line falls between justified response and anti-democratic exploitation. Some of the countries that have been most successful at flattening the curve have deployed aggressive contact tracing techniques that, on their face, would violate civil rights.

Israeli prime minister Benjamin Netanyahu authorized the use of invasive cellphone location tracking, intended for counterterrorism, to track those who test positive for the virus and monitor others with whom they may have come into contact. The South Korean government's policy of releasing detailed information including the names and movements of newly diagnosed cases has inadvertently revealed sexual affairs and other embarrassing personal information.

What's more, even well-established democracies are flirting with injustice. Despite pleas from the Democratic governor of Wisconsin, the

Republican-dominated legislature, abetted by the state Supreme Court, has used the crisis to play partisan politics. In recent voting, it refused to extend the window for mail-in ballots and reduced the number of polling stations in the state from 180 to five, all of which were conveniently located in areas that lean Republican.

As the curve is flattened and the threat of the virus recedes, it remains to be seen how many of these unjust measures will be repealed. The last time Orbán awarded himself extraordinary powers under the guise of an emergency—powers he has yet to relinquish—it was the 2011 migrant crisis.

What every strongman has understood, from Cecil to Orbán, is that a frightened public is also a compliant public. For the sake of our democracy, our leaders must understand that while we are willing to be compliant, to do our duty, to surrender some of our individual rights and liberties for the collective good, we are not frightened. Not in the least.

THOUGHT-PROVOKING

In my line of work, I see it all the time. Businesses forget who they are and what value they deliver. Public figures lose their North Star and disconnect from their base. Which is why, one month into lockdown, in the midst of a collective crisis, I asked about Canadian society's most essential feature—our democracy.

History teaches us that extraordinary measures require extraordinary oversight. Governments use crises as pretexts to seize new levels of authority they may, eventually, refuse to relinquish. And in fact, we saw Viktor Orbán in Hungary and Rodrigo Duterte in the Philippines use the pandemic as an excuse to expand their authoritarian powers and agenda.

In short, I got this column right.

I wonder today how history will judge the actions and inactions of certain governments during the pandemic.

Even if you're in the camp of those who believe governments did too little (a camp that does not include me), you must admit it's imperative we assess those most disturbing incidents when governments overreached. Understanding where the line rests between justified measures and anti-democratic exploitation is tough. But here's the thing: crises that surface these precise questions are not going anywhere.

In contrast with the authoritarians whose overreaches I cited above are those whom we can draw lessons from to battle the next pandemic. In Germany, former chancellor Angela Merkel got it right. Though her government implemented strict lockdowns, they also offered strong economic supports to citizens and have been widely praised for the transparency of their communications. The same can be said for South Korea.

As the *Washington Post's* famous slogan declares, "Democracy dies in the darkness." For me, that darkness consists—in part—in a failure to engage one another respectfully on the hardest questions. Look, it's not easy to know when repealed liberties are for the collective good or when they're a perilous step across the line toward authoritarianism. So let's not be too fearful to seriously reflect on when and how our own governments crossed the line, or too lethargic to examine those instances in which they got things right.

May 24, 2020

Most workers in Canadian long-term care facilities—a group uniquely
vulnerable to the spread of COVID-19—are women.
But the fact is, these issues did not arrive with COVID-19,
nor will they disappear with a vaccine.

The "She-cession" May Be New, But Its Underlying Causes Are Not

O f all the inequalities laid bare by the COVID-19 pandemic, there is none more glaring than the profoundly unequal effect it has had on the lives of women.

The impacts are felt everywhere. Primary caregivers have been forced to balance their professional and personal lives like never before, as children stay home from school and work comes home. The psychological and financial pressures of the pandemic have exacerbated the conditions for domestic violence, which impacts Canadian women at a disproportionate rate. Most workers in Canadian long-term care facilities—a group uniquely vulnerable to the spread of COVID-19—are women.

But the fact is, these issues did not arrive with COVID-19, nor will they disappear with a vaccine.

First, the role of women at home. As we look ahead to the reopening of our economy, the wildly unequal division of labour in most households, along with the expected phased nature of reopening, will pose additional challenges for women seeking to return to work.

While some daycares in Ontario have reopened, schools and camps will be closed until the fall. How can we expect parents to return to work without any feasible options for child care?

Second, in public health terms, women face a crisis with unequal repercussions. Over 50 percent of Canada's COVID-19 cases and deaths are women, making us an exception among nations where the prevailing trend is one of majority-male cases. The apparent reasons are that Canadian women live longer than men and many high-risk jobs (like long-term care work) are done by women. But the trend is disturbing, nonetheless.

And third, there is the troublingly unequal economic impact for women. Unlike previous recessions that have mostly impacted goods-producing sectors, COVID-19's devastation has been largely focused on the service economy.

In the 2008-2009 recession, widespread hits to manufacturing and construction meant that a male workforce bore the brunt of the downturn. But, this time out, rather than job sites and warehouses, it is hospitality and retail that are hurting most. As a result, the majority of jobs lost due to COVID-19, in both Canada and the United States, have been held by women. From mid-February to mid-March, nearly 62 percent of Canadian job losses were experienced by women.

But those numbers hide an even more significant challenge. Many of those women were let go earlier than their male counterparts and their return to the workplace will be a more significant uphill battle.

It's now clear that what we face in 2020 is not simply a recession but a "she-cession"; one that will impact the economic life of women in a very unequal way.

So what does this mean? It means our governments need to ditch the playbook they used in 2008-2009 and create one that responds to the needs of this particular crisis.

And they have begun to do just that. So far, Trudeau and his cabinet have shown a promising commitment to addressing some of the issues facing women across Canada: fifty million dollars has been provided for services that support women, children, and victims of assault. Last week, Minister Mary Ng announced a fifteen-million-dollar investment to help female business owners through the pandemic. The augmented Canada child benefit announced by the prime minister this week is another step in the right direction.

But compare this to more than $280 billion in overall COVID-19 relief and the case is made that much, much more is needed.

And there are other considerations. Rather than simply focusing on social supports and targeted pandemic spending, the Trudeau government must take a holistic approach that considers the role of women in our wider economic recovery. That means proper tools to track and analyze the unique impact of this crisis along gender lines as well as innovative options for bolstering our service economy to ensure that unemployment trends no longer impact female earners so profoundly. It also means a genuine commitment to tackle the gender inequalities that predate COVID-19 but have been exacerbated by the pandemic.

Getting this right—resolving our systematic challenges as well as our temporal ones—will allow us to come out of this crisis as a stronger, more caring, and more successful country.

INSPIRED

Some good news for a change. As I write this book, we're starting to see signs of a "she-covery." In 2021, according to economist Armine Yalnizyan, who coined the term "she-cession," more than 1.5 million women were out of work.[60] By January 2023, the number of women aged twenty-five to fifty-four in the workforce grew by 51,000, pushing the women's employment rate up to 82 percent—its highest since 1976.

Just one example of the shrewd policy underlying this turnaround is the ten-dollars-a-day subsidized child-care program, announced by the federal Liberals in 2021. Mothers will no longer have to sacrifice entire paycheques for daycare. I'm particularly proud of this achievement because the team at Navigator helped champion it.

When it comes to gender equality, lip service abounds, but concrete steps are often lacking. While I highlighted the main barriers facing women and called for holistic approaches, I wish I'd also identified solutions. If you'll permit me a mulligan, here's what those steps could look like.

First, we must tackle gender-based violence. One horrifying aspect of the pandemic was growing rates of sexual assault, femicide, and family violence enabled by the lockdowns. Approximately every six days, a woman in Canada is killed by her intimate partner.[61] Policymakers must work alongside experts in the third sector like the Canadian Women's Foundation, who provide services like housing and crisis support, emergency shelter, child-witness-to-violence programs, and healthy-relationship education for teens. As we've learned in recent years, those working on the front lines know best.

Second, let's support the most vulnerable women, including disabled women and single mothers with young children. With inflation rising, they need affordable essentials and economic stimulus.

Third, we should acknowledge that the fight for gender equality isn't over. Far too few cis and trans women, trans men, Two-Spirit, and nonbinary people are in leadership roles. One step would be to clamp down on the online harassment that dissuades people of marginalized genders from entering public life.

While the pandemic was catastrophic, it shone a light on some of our most glaring public-policy gaps. This is one of them.

June 13, 2020

Terrified of losing their moral authority to govern, their power of moral suasion, the tail is, once again, wagging the dog with public health authorities repeatedly contorting themselves or playing catch-up to shifts of opinion and behaviour among the public.

We Are Done with COVID-19, But It Is Not Done With Us

Though it now seems easy to forget, we remain locked in a battle with the novel coronavirus. It has been ninety-three days since the World Health Organization declared COVID-19 a pandemic, a declaration that brought with it unprecedented restrictions on our liberties and to our livelihoods.

That we all willingly obeyed those orders is a notion fundamental to a democratic society: the consent of the citizen to submit to the authority of the government.

But the mass protests of past weeks have shown a fraying of this social contract. Prompted by an angry outcry to a long-simmering wrong, the Black Lives Matter movement has caught on where the anti-lockdown movement has fizzled out.

The BLM protests are, as I wrote here last week, justified and long overdue and the anti-quarantine movement was never more than a radical fringe. But the outcome and the dangers, vis-à-vis the coronavirus, are much the same.

While it is dangerous to confuse the real medical risk of these protests with their ideological or political value, we have seen public health authorities trip over themselves to somehow sanction them. They seem suddenly desperate to inoculate themselves against the criticism that it remains irresponsible to gather in large groups, even outdoors, even in a mask.

It was just a month ago that irresponsibility was the charge levelled against those who protested the COVID-19 lockdowns. It was only two weeks ago that health and political authorities alike were condemning youth in Trinity Bellwoods Park, going so far as to label them reckless and selfish.

But governments have now run into a brick wall when it comes to public compliance. Terrified of losing their moral authority to govern, their power of moral suasion, the tail is, once again, wagging the dog with public health authorities repeatedly contorting themselves or playing catch-up to shifts of opinion and behaviour among the public.

As the social contract frays, the more pronounced this phenomenon becomes, and the more the authority of government will erode.

Public health authorities can issue endless reminders about best practices but now that every leader from the prime minister on down has participated in a mass gathering, the government's dissuasive power against gathering in large groups has melted like a Popsicle in the summer sun.

This fraying will only get worse, I predict. Whether it is because of the warm weather, general quarantine fatigue after three long months, or deteriorating mental or financial health, people are simply ceasing to do what the government asks.

And why should they? It is not as if our leaders have modelled good behaviour. If others are not willing to follow the basic rules of the social contract, it is rather easy to understand those who choose to abandon quarantine to join a growing popular protest movement. After all, condemning untold instances of appalling police brutality seems to many a reasonable and necessary thing to do.

Public health authorities like Dr. Anthony Fauci are, of course, of a different view. Dr. Fauci sternly warned this week that the protests are the "perfect set-up" for spreading the virus. The challenge for governments is that it will take a couple of weeks to see if he is right. And while we wait, it will be difficult for authorities to convince the public that the risk is real when Toronto public health authorities recently quietly confirmed that we saw no such spike after the gathering in Bellwoods.

And so, it is becoming clear that we have collectively decided that, regardless of what we are told, we are done with COVID-19.

But the virus is not done with us—far from it.

And therein lies the challenge facing those who lead our democracy.

What happens when the people decide they have had enough? What happens when the people decide that they will no longer blindly, unquestioningly accept instructions? What happens when science and instinct and experience lead you in one direction and the people lead you in another?

Those are questions that will preoccupy our leaders through the doldrums of summer. And their answers will live on much longer in the health of our nation and the political fortunes of their parties.

EXPECT THE UNEXPECTED

To answer my own question: *democratic backsliding*, or the slow erosion of democratic characteristics, norms, and ideas within a country. That's what happens when people abandon science out of desperation to regain their perceived freedoms—whether they've truly been taken away or not. Look no further than the Capitol riots in the US. Though primarily motivated by false claims of a "stolen" election, many in that crowd were violently opposed to public health measures. In Canada, the smaller-scale "Freedom Convoy" incident was symptomatic of similar feelings from that far-right sect of the public, evolving into outright resistance that was only subdued by the Emergencies Act.[62]

While I was right about the general frustration with the pandemic measures, I was wrong about the extent to which Canadians would consistently—through so many peaks and valleys—follow public health advice. A vast majority of Canadians complied, from masking mandates to vaccines to gathering limits, for as long as these health mandates were in place.

Those who didn't were small in number but extremely loud. A group that not only turned on the government but on their fellow citizens. Not coincidentally, there's been an increase in violence in our cities since the public health restrictions were lifted. People are more divided than ever, due in no small part to the social separation that came about because of disparate reactions to the health measures.

Democratic backsliding, like what we have seen in the United States, is the ultimate result of this ideological division. Trump and his cronies seized on a divided public, distress-stricken by the pandemic, and used the opportunity to try to usurp American democracy. Let's count ourselves lucky that they were too disorganized on January 6. It is obvious, however, that they won't stop until their small minority has complete power. Trump's indictment won't change that. Canada must take the United States' situation as a dire warning to de-radicalize our politics and go back to being the boring upstairs neighbour we were always meant to be. The brass tacks? Most of us here are pretty good about following rules.

October 25, 2020

Since March, the story of Canada's pandemic response has been one of unprecedented teamwork between different parties and levels of government. There have been tensions in Ottawa but for the most part, the Liberals have been able to rely on NDP and Green support to pass their COVID-19 agenda. However, this week marked a definite turn toward a more confrontational style of governing by the prime minister and his cabinet.

After an Unseasonably Cooperative Summer, the Chill of Realpolitik Is Settling In

As the warmth of summer has faded and the chill of fall set in, we have felt a similar change in temperature in legislatures across Canada. From the House of Commons to Queen's Park to the Legislative Assembly of Alberta and the National Assembly of Quebec. From provincial capitals to city halls, the tone of pandemic politics has shifted significantly. After seven months of relatively cordial, pragmatic, and co-operative policy-making, it seems the time for playing "patty-cake" across the aisle has passed. Welcome back to reality.

Since March, the story of Canada's pandemic response has been one of unprecedented teamwork between different parties and levels of government. To be sure, there have been tensions in Ottawa, but for the most part, the Liberals have been able to rely on NDP and Green support to pass their COVID-19 agenda. But let's not assign either party too many brownie points. Neither could afford the consequences of not supporting the government: an election.

However, this week marked a definite turn toward a more confrontational style of governing by the prime minister and his cabinet. Facing the prospect of new Opposition-led oversight efforts, Trudeau and Liberal House Leader Pablo Rodriguez launched a game of high-stakes chicken.

By daring opposition parties to trigger an election, the Liberals have shown they are not afraid to play hardball to avoid legislative paralysis-by-investigation. In so doing, they've also made it clear they don't intend to water down their pandemic plans to please their opponents in the House. So until the NDP and the Greens decide they have had enough, we can expect the partisan brawling to get even messier. So long, sunny ways.

Across the country, a similar process is taking place as political leaders eschew COVID co-operation in favour of closing ranks and turning on their would-be partners.

In British Columbia, Premier John Horgan was quick to turn on the BC Greens who have supported his government since 2017. Not only did the premier renege on his pledge to avoid an early trip to the polls, he's also laid blame for the election on the other parties. Whether you view Horgan's decision as necessary pragmatism or opportunistic overreach, his motive is clear: to exploit a pandemic opportunity to sideline his opponents and implement his agenda, his way.

And then there is the most improbable of COVID-induced friendships: the Ontario Conservatives and the federal Liberals. Last spring, Premier Ford and Deputy Prime Minister Chrystia Freeland made the strangest of bedfellows. Ford called Freeland "amazing." She said, "He's my therapist." Now, even that relationship is being tested.

After the Liberals' throne speech, Ford expressed his disappointment at Ottawa's reluctance to invest its "fair share" in health care. The premier has also accused Ottawa of being too lax with quarantine restrictions and has repeatedly criticized Health Canada for delays in testing across the province.

The awkwardness of this post-honeymoon phase crystallized in a joint announcement by the prime minister and Premier Ford, when the two leaders were asked what had changed in their previously rocky relationship. Ever the realist, Ford's assessment of the political reality was very straightforward: "A big chunk of them that voted for the prime minister, voted for me. People expect us to work together."

Ford's right: Ontarians want him to work with the prime minister, and with his favourability numbers sliding, the premier would be wise to listen. But that co-operation will become more difficult as the second wave worsens, and provincial and federal priorities diverge.

And as we saw with Ford's initial disagreements over indoor dining with Dr. Eileen de Villa, Toronto's medical officer of health, it is one thing to mend over political disagreements and coalesce around a scientific consensus. It is another thing entirely to find common ground when the nuances in different public health advice leave room for disagreement.

For all of us, pandemic fatigue will grow worse as the days grow shorter. For our politicians, they will grow fatigued with getting along with their natural opponents.

The problem is, this COVID thing isn't over. We all have to put our big kid pants on and keep our fatigue in check.

Regrettably, it took me to the end of the piece to get to the meat of the issue: that honeymoons between different orders of government invariably come to a bitter end.

At the pandemic's outset, governing parties got a boost from "rallying around the flag." Then, as crisis fatigue set in, voters became increasingly upset with government performance. The blame game began.

Hubert Humphrey, who served as LBJ's vice-president, once said, "To err is human. To blame someone else is politics."[63]

Nowhere does the act of assigning blame have a more mountain-out of-a-molehill quality than in politics. Here, blame is assigned at every turn, for every misdeed. Then come the blame-avoidance tactics. One fuels the other. This vicious cycle metastasizes, destroying cohesion and efficiency.

In short, everybody's too busy levelling accusations or covering their ass to get anything done.

The different orders of government behave this way for good reason. In our system, politics is a zero-sum game. In order to win, someone else needs to lose. Or, at least, that's how it is played today.

The consequences can be summarized as follows: *blame oversaturation*. The public hears so many accusations and counter-accusations fly around that they cease to hold any meaning. These cases generally produce two outcomes.

First, all governing parties involved in a given issue equally take a hit in the polls. The recent issue of rising crime in Toronto is a prime example. The municipal, provincial, and federal government are all being challenged by the public and their political opponents for not doing enough.[64] All three orders stand to suffer in the polls.

Second, when the blame game's musical chairs come to an abrupt halt, one order is left without a seat. Standing there, they must absorb *all* the blame. There's no better recent illustration of this phenomenon than mayors countrywide absorbing significant political damage for the affordable-housing crisis.[65] [66] Obviously, municipal governments alone cannot fix this issue. And yet, since they're perceived to be the most directly responsible, incumbent mayors and councillors are struggling as a result. It might be unfair, but that's the risk of playing.

December 20, 2020

*We do not yet know how dire things may become this winter. There may
come a time when another round of emergency relief will be needed.
And if that day comes, I bet we'll be glad for Ford and his
long view of Ontario's finances.*

We May Yet Be Thankful for "Premier Scrooge"

L ast week, Ontario's Financial Accountability Office came out with another report, this one finding twelve billion dollars in COVID funds apparently unspent by the province. This latest report, which looked at the second quarter, follows on a previous first-quarter FAO report that found the province had $6.7 billion in unspent pandemic funds.

Both reports predictably spawned days, even weeks, of breathless sound bites on radio and television, tut-tut editorials in newspapers and smart-ass quips on social media.

"MPPs should be staying at the legislature and working to use the twelve billion dollars in COVID funding Doug Ford has been withholding from the people of Ontario," tweeted Opposition Leader Andrea Horwath, before Queen's Park rose for the holiday break.

Bereft of an imagination and resorting to the most tiresome cliché, the Liberals shared a graphic that labelled Doug Ford "Premier Scrooge." Steven Del Duca, their leader, charged that the premier had "hoarded twelve billion dollars in funding that should have been used to save lives," and asked, "How can Doug Ford justify this callous budgeting to families who've lost a parent or grandparent to COVID-19?"

The problem with this criticism of the Ford government's pandemic response spending is that it is both short-sighted and fiscally reckless. Would Horwath and Del Duca prefer the government to have spent the entire envelope in the first leg of what everyone knows will be a marathon journey?

Surely no Ontario family that spent all of their reserve funds within the first or second quarter of the pandemic would be applauding themselves for responsible financial management. And they certainly wouldn't be applauding a government that did the same.

Far from sitting atop these funds like Smaug, as the Opposition would have you believe, the Ford government has already allocated 80 percent of the funds in question through its budget. While these allocations might shift, as the pandemic elevates new priorities and presents new challenges, at least the province has delivered a budget. That's more than can be said for the federal Liberals, who (like many other provincial governments) have relied on vague economic updates to outline their spending plans.

This partisan criticism of Ontario's spending does us no favours. What we really need now, as a province and as a country, is an honest year-end conversation about the fiscal impact of COVID-19.

In that regard, financial accountability officer Peter Weltman is deserving of praise—his reports are insightful precisely because of their narrow focus. His conduct stands in stark contrast to the auditor general, whose mission creep and general inability to stay in her lane has been well-covered in the pages of this newspaper.

All public servants whose job it is to account for the expenditure of public funds will, appropriately, be under scrutiny in the time ahead. Statistically speaking, some degree of fraud, mismanagement, abuse, or cronyism is inevitable. After all, in an astonishingly short window of time, COVID has resulted in the biggest outlays of government spending in memory. The province has spent (or plans to spend) some forty-five billion dollars on COVID-related issues, while the feds have spent more than $322 billion in related relief.

But even as Ford is condemned for underspending, the federal government is finding that as they go, they may have overspent or under-projected. Already the $322 billion sum is more than double the figure projected at the outset of the pandemic in March.

And just this week, the federal parliamentary budget officer (PBO) found that some of Ottawa's signature COVID-relief programs, such as the emergency wage subsidy, will turn out to be vastly more expensive than anticipated. In the fall economic update, Finance Minister Chrystia Freeland predicted the subsidy would cost some $16.2 billion. The PBO has revised that number upward to $85.5 billion.

This most recent episode helpfully illustrates the sensibility of the Ford government's approach. After all, we do not yet know how dire things may become this winter. If a further lockdown is ultimately warranted, or the current regional lockdown is extended interminably, there may come a time when another round of emergency relief will be needed. And if that day comes, I bet we'll be glad for Premier Scrooge and his long view of Ontario's finances.

ON THE SCENT

This column holds more than meets the eye.

On the surface, it covers familiar dynamics. A right-wing government exercises fiscal restraint, while a left-wing opposition calls for greater spending, which they paint as desperately needed.

Upon closer examination, this story's different. Just look at the numbers. They're worth returning to now with greater perspective.

In 2020-2021, federal government spending increased by 73 percent,[67] and total spending by all levels of government reached an all-time high of over one trillion dollars,[68] a number so big, it defies Canadian comparison. It's a figure I thought we were a long way off from seeing here in our fake G7 economy.

If these aren't paradigm-altering figures, I can't imagine what are.

So, while I applauded the Ford government for striving to maintain fiscal sanity, I should have taken a wider lens and underlined for my readers that what constitutes "sanity" had, critically, been redrawn.

For the better part of a century, fiscal restraint and "balancing the budget" have been central to conservative party brands nationwide. What happens when that mission becomes impossible, not just within government mandates but across generations?

Thus far, we've seen conservative politicians focus on waste. And with good reason. The 2022 auditor general's report found that billions of COVID spending was either entirely wasted or poorly targeted.[69]

But here's the curiosity. Present those numbers to the Canadian public a decade ago and it would have produced an uncontrollable political shitstorm. Today, you might get an angry op-ed in the *National Post*.

Clearly, the brand needs repositioning. Our new fiscal reality demands Conservatives offer a new narrative, one that conveys they're a party that can make government work *better* for Canadians. Put it this way. No one buys a car exclusively for the price. Even buyers on a budget require performance and dependability. Whatever the bumpy road ahead might hold, big government is here to stay. Conservatives must do more than claim they can shrink it.

It's a test Doug Ford met. And if he ever becomes prime minister, it's a test that Pierre Poilievre will no doubt face.

January 10, 2021

During the HIV/AIDS crisis, we learned that shame served to drive the virus further underground, making it harder to monitor and treat. With COVID, epidemiologists say that condemnations should be reserved for broad categories of behaviour—mass indoor gatherings, say, or mid-winter tropical vacations, and not individuals who may transgress.

Accountability Is Crucial, But Public Shaming Only Makes Things Worse

As the pandemic explodes into the new year, the roller coaster of emotions we all are experiencing continues.

We have been afraid as we confronted an unknown virus, and we continue to be afraid. We have felt guilty as we wondered what more we could do to help friends, colleagues, or neighbours get through these difficult times, and we continue to feel guilty. We have clung to hope that a vaccine will be our answer, and we cling to that hope still.

But these past weeks have been dominated by a singular and all-too-familiar emotional dynamic: shame.

Long before we began our ongoing witch hunt against any politician or public figure who has stepped foot outside the country during the pandemic, there were previous instances of public shaming over the course of COVID-19.

Recall the *Toronto Sun* cover ("COVIDIOTS") shaming the summertime gathering of youths in Trinity Bellwoods. Or the case of a doctor in Nova Scotia who travelled over the border to Quebec to retrieve his daughter, and faced horrifically racist recriminations when he returned and inadvertently infected a patient.

Never mind the fact that the day in the park caused no discernable spike in cases, or the fact that the doctor was told by authorities to return to work in the first place—the public shaming came just the same.

The longer that all this wears on, the more tempting it becomes to resort to this crude form of social pressure. We are in a strict lockdown, but the number of cases continues to rise. Therefore, many have concluded that people must be breaking the rules—and rulebreakers deserve to be named and shamed.

What's more, we have new tools for that shaming. Where once we shamed people in the public square, in newspapers, or on television, we now take to social media, where the cycle of recriminations has been turbocharged.

So we must ask ourselves: In a pandemic, is shame a useful form of public pressure? Some observers say yes—merely the possibility of a public shaming is enough to dissuade undesirable behaviour.

But if we are truly to allow ourselves to be guided by the science, and if the academic research is to be believed, the answer is a sturdy no. In study after study of pandemics or epidemics past—from obesity to fetal alcohol syndrome—researchers have found shaming tactics or techniques result in health outcomes that are *worse*.

As a gay man who survived the HIV/AIDS pandemic of the 1980s and 1990s, I am well-versed in these arguments and rationales. How long did it take us to learn that to stigmatize those with HIV only dissuades potential cases from getting tested and, if positive, from making responsible choices about their status? Shame serves to drive the virus further underground, and that makes it harder to monitor and treat.

But shaming carriers of contagious disease has a long history (going all the way back to Typhoid Mary), and the impulses behind it are not so easy to wrestle down with logic. It's simple enough now to explain why shaming HIV-positive people is counterproductive, but with COVID-19, the epidemiology of the virus has been in a constant state of flux. The rules and recommendations protecting us against it are vague and necessarily iterative.

The bottom line is that it is easier to shame individuals for perceived lapses or shortcomings than it is to really grapple with this uncertainty, or to rise above it. We resort to shame because it is easier to point the finger than to offer a solution or extend a hand.

Ten months of trying to harass individual people into compliance has clearly failed. By now, we must understand that infection is not a moral failure, and that all individuals will make their own risk calculations under the guidelines and regulations set forward by governments.

Disagreements abound, but there is a better way. Expert epidemiologists say that condemnations should be reserved for broad categories of behaviour—mass indoor gatherings, say, or mid-winter tropical vacations, and not individuals who may transgress. In short, as we look ahead to the end of this wretched pandemic, we need to learn to hate the sin, and not the sinner.

TOO NAIVE

The maxim I close with, "Hate the sin, and not the sinner," comes from Gandhi. The full quote from his 1929 autobiography clarifies: "Though easy enough to understand, [this precept] is rarely practised, and that is why the poison of hatred spreads in the world."[70]

Throughout the pandemic, we saw much worse than the acts of public shaming I describe in this column. Empowered by the anonymity of the Internet, we saw many people celebrating, outright, the deaths of their fellow citizens. The best-known example of this depressing phenomenon was the popular subreddit "Herman Cain Award." Named after the former GOP presidential candidate who died from COVID-19 after publicly refusing to wear a mask, in this sad, sardonic corner of the web, followers celebrate the virus-related deaths of those who'd made known their anti-mask, anti-vax, or Covid-hoax views.

Schadenfreude scarcely covers this wickedness. And the phenomenon actually went both ways. Many in the anti-vax community harassed those who closely observed public health directives.

The pandemic created conditions whereby normal citizens were socially conditioned to see those who held different views from their own as subhuman. What can be done to avoid such hostile behaviour again? For me, it starts with preventing the rampant spread of fear. It's in climates of generalized dread and confusion that we see the worst human instincts kick in. Of course, fear proportionate to the threat of both the virus and of the socio-economic risks involved with an indefinitely shut-down society were warranted. And yet, during the COVID-19 pandemic, the distressing social epidemics of fear, stigmatization, and extreme polarization must serve as a reminder to governments and public health officials that fear is an extremely dangerous tool that must be employed (if at all) with the utmost caution.

Benjamin Franklin said, "Those who would give up essential liberty to purchase a little temporary safety deserve neither liberty nor safety."[71] The following question was the crux of many a pandemic-era debate: What constitutes "*essential* liberty" on the one hand, and "temporary safety" on the other?

If you are familiar with the "lab leak" hypothesis of COVID's beginnings, it may be as a fringe conspiracy theory that was quickly dismissed. Suddenly, however, everyone from Science Magazine to the US intelligence community is reconsidering the idea.

How Media's Groupthink Effect Led to Bungling of COVID's Origin Story

As the end of the pandemic mercifully nears, everything old is becoming new again. Nowhere is that more evident than in the ongoing debate—revisionist history and all—over the origins of COVID-19.

You may already be familiar with the widely accepted version of the story, which involves animal-to-human transmission beginning in or around a wet market in Wuhan.[72]

If you are familiar at all with the competing "lab leak" hypothesis,[73] it may be as a fringe conspiracy, parroted by a certain former president and peddled by the likes of Fox News. Recent events, however, have helped return this idea from the fringe to the mainstream.

The lab-leak theory holds that the virus may have escaped from the Wuhan Institute of Virology. When this theory was originally posited, it was based on the idea of an accident. But in the frenzied political environment that was early 2020, the story morphed in some tellings such that China had released COVID as a bioweapon—a manifestly ridiculous idea that was all too easy to dismiss.

But there is now a reappraisal of the original lab-leak hypothesis. Suddenly, everyone from *Science* magazine to the US intelligence community is reconsidering the idea.

Needless to say, I am no expert, and the question of COVID's true origins won't be solved in this column. Actual experts, who have laid out convincing bodies of evidence on both sides, will sort it out.

But I am interested in the question of why we were so blind to this possibility in the first place, and just why the mainstream media has such a tough time which stories like this—ones that involve some degree of uncertainty.

To process these stories, we fall back on a collective obsession with fact-checking, lie-counting, and sorting every political statement into tidy categories of True or False in response.

It's an approach may have served us well when an inveterate liar occupied the White House, but this model has floundered during the COVID-19 pandemic. Doctors and scientists simply have tools and techniques to understand this virus that are not available to the public.

That is why, as far back as a year and a half ago, scientists like Dr. Alina Chan at Harvard were discussing the lab leak as a viable hypothesis.

But because the theory's political messengers came from the right, including Senator Tom Cotton and former president Donald Trump, the theory was distorted and then dismissed as a dangerous lie or conspiracy theory.

Politifact rated the idea "pants on fire"[74] and the other so-called fact-checking outlets followed suit. Recently, many of them have been forced to issue retractions, but the media's powerful groupthink effect was already hard at work.

Scientists who backed the wet-market theory were spotlighted and booked on TV; scientists who were skeptical of it were shunned and silenced on social media.

This had the overall effect of making it seem as if a scientific consensus existed, when in fact there was none. Rather, it was simply the media's perverse incentive structure at work.

Once again, helped along by political polarization, public opinion calcified in a way that was exceedingly unhelpful.

In part, this debacle is a lesson in politics and the dangers of polarization, which can clearly blind us to important lines of inquiry. Progressives, who were rightfully concerned with the rise of anti-Asian hate crimes, dismissed the idea out of hand for all the wrong reasons. At the same time, politicians like Trump or Cotton, who have built their careers on xenophobia and general dishonesty, make it virtually impossible to take anything they say in good faith.

Part of this debacle is also a lesson in humility, especially for those of us in the media who prognosticate for a living. The industrial fact-checking complex should be scaled back in favour of reporting that helps the public to understand the complexities inherent to these issues.

When it comes to COVID-19's origins, the truth of the matter may never be known, thanks in large part to China's obfuscation and the WHO's shameful acceptance thereof.

But the rest of us need not be blind forever—unless, of course, we choose to.

ON POINT

Recent developments have only made this column more poignant.

In 2023, the US Department of Energy announced the "lab leak" hypothesis was the most likely origin of COVID-19.[75] In this assessment, they joined the FBI and several other agencies.

This development hasn't stopped proponents on either side of this debate from running around in circles like two defiant children.

Child One, let's call him Conspiracy Carl, is dancing victory laps, taunting his opponents at every turn. Child Two, let's call her Cautious Candice, is sticking to her guns and still dismisses this hypothesis as a racist ploy.

What both these toddlers need is a time out and a stern talking to.

Let's start with Conspiracy Carl. First, Carl, you should know that the matter is hardly closed. Other US agencies and voices of authority still hold the virus arose from a "natural" development. But if you really want to insist you've won, then repeating the sins of your opponent by labelling them with terms like "woke idealogues" won't help. Nor will it help distance you from the genuine racists who celebrated your position. For you, the only logical path forward is to exercise humility. Try it on. It'll do wonders for your blood pressure.

Don't think you're getting off the hook, Cautious Candice. You, of all people, should know that in genuine science, disagreement and uncertainty are part of the process. Dismissing possibilities out of hand and branding all who entertain alternative avenues as "bigots" is not. By the way, don't you think that by insisting the "lab leak" was a conspiracy, only for that "conspiracy" to look increasingly true, might've helped lend credence to actual conspiracies?

Time out's over. This is something for both of you to hear: clearly, we are aiming to walk a fine line between permitting hate speech and racist conspiracies to spiral and suppressing valid discussion by reacting to polarization with social censure and intolerance.

We'll never find that line if denigration is the end goal of every political inquiry. No. It must be truth, inconvenient and prone to fluctuation as it might be.

Epilogue

One Last Thing

When I first started writing columns, I never wrote in the first-person per-spective, never used "I." I thought that using the first-person was presump-tuous, boastful. At lunch with my editor one day, he explained that I was wrong. Dead wrong. He explained that readers wanted to be let inside my life, and that I should get comfortable with that. In striving to follow his advice, I realized that I had previously attempted to mask myself with words rather than take full ownership for what I was trying to say.

In finding and arranging these columns, I was looking to do just that: take ownership. Reading the best was easy. The worst, well, not so much.

I knew there would be awkwardness in dealing with past positions. And I felt that awkwardness—unquestionably. But I'm not one to moan and protest about the past. I instead chose to think of those misfires as part of an inescapable process. Before long, my unease simply melted away, and I found that my precious sense of pride and vanity had vanished too.

Surprisingly, it was in writing *What I Wish I Said* that I quickly learned that my poorest columns were the richest in ammunition. It was these that I was the most enthusiastic about—absolutely determined to get right, to not make a mess out of the second time around.

And so, I had to find my own way and chart my own path. As I reviewed all the work over those years, I also came to experience the process of writing this book as a form of self-examination. I came to know myself on a deeper level, beyond those vague memories of frantically writing at my desk early Friday morning.

The truth is that I had no idea how sick I was when I wrote most of these columns. I don't think it is random that now, with a feeling of new-found well-being, I was truly ready to have an honest look at my body of work.

In the process, I came to understand that column writing is not as solitary as it sometimes feels. Rather, it is a little bit like cooking a meal. You prepare it by yourself, but you share it with others. And it is in the act of sharing that I've learned the most.

I understand today that people are reading my column for a reason—because they want to hear from *me*. So, today, I never shy away from the opportunity to assert my voice. To let readers know that they're hearing from me and no one else. Hearing not just my point of view—but what I care about.

So, I'd like to close with the column that has garnered one of the largest reactions in recent memory.

March 5, 2023

If the headline didn't already give it away, well then—spoiler alert—this column takes a wide turn from the politics I usually write about, to the personal, which I seldom do.

How an Organ Donation Saved My Life

A year ago I had a kidney transplant.

Since then, my life has changed in ways I never dreamt possible. To be able to dream of something, you must be able to imagine it. But I could never have imagined my life today, much less dreamt of it. In fact, I have no memory of feeling this good.

Before my surgery, I had been living with end-stage kidney disease. And like many other illnesses that develop over time, you get used to things being just as they are. But with kidney disease, you eventually get to a very bad place. A place where you are faced with three options: do nothing and die, undergo dialysis, or get a new kidney.

And so while it is a surprise to many, a transplant is the treatment of choice for this disease. And that's what I was blessed enough to have.

In every respect, I won the lottery of life. My partner and I were a match. I live in Toronto—the best place, on the evidence, on the planet to have your kidney transplanted. And our Medicare system ensured I wouldn't be wiped out financially.

Fortunate as I was, many are not. According to Canadian Blood Services, over four thousand Canadians are waiting for not just a life-saving, but a life-transforming, organ transplant. And this is no comfortable "wait." People really suffer; their lives deteriorate daily. And most tragically of all, the most unnecessary and painful fact is that—each year—for hundreds of our fellow citizens time runs out and they die while waiting.

The reason for this is no mystery: there are simply not enough organs to meet the demand. And the solution is not a mystery either.

International comparisons show that Canada's donor rates are significantly lower than the United States, Spain, and France. And I can't imagine there is a Canadian among us who thinks that's okay.

The good news is the path forward has been discovered, tried, and tested here in Canada. The approach is what's known as presumed organ consent (or "opt out" legislation). In short, this means people are presumed to consent to donate their organs after their death unless they opt out.

In 2021, Nova Scotia became the first jurisdiction in North America to adopt this practice, and it's already saving lives. But the policy rationale extends beyond life-saving potential. People who require organ donation depend heavily on our medical system for vital care and support.

Indeed, dialysis costs roughly one hundred thousand dollars a year per patient in Canada.[76] By comparison, a transplant costs approximately $66,000 with continuing costs of roughly $23,000 per year for monitoring and anti-rejection medications. These are not insignificant savings for an already overburdened sector.

There are, of course, many ethical dilemmas to navigate on this issue and any future plans must guarantee that religious and spiritual convictions are respected. However, the "opt out" policy option is a proven solution. One that saves lives. It is also a solution that matches the incredible compassion and generosity of the Canadian people.

In the late Paul Dewar's final statement to Canadians, he told us he saw his illness as a gift. I never truly understood his words until I was lying by myself in an ICU bed with an IV in each arm.

But now, I do.

The finest gifts fill you with a sense of awe, humility, renewed purpose. Today, I have a *new* life because the man I love risked his own. You can't quantify this feeling of gratitude. Or touch it. Or hold it in your hand.

You can live out your life with humility and renewed purpose and awe. You can give back and tell your story. You can keep the gift alive.

Enough said.

Afterword

In Conversation with Michael Cooke

Throughout this book, I've effectively been talking to myself—albeit my past self. Believe me, it's been an enlightening, sobering, and sometimes humbling exercise. I found myself wishing I *hadn't* said certain things. Indeed, I've learned more about my shortcomings as a writer and pundit through this experience than I have since, well, I started as a columnist seven years ago. But I would be fooling myself if I didn't acknowledge that I am just beginning to get the hang of this thing.

Time for an outside voice, *another perspective.*

And there's none better than the former editor of the *Toronto Star* and current chair of the Board of Journalists for Human Rights, Michael Cooke. Michael was the *Star's* longest-serving editor-in-chief in recent history, presiding from 2009–2018.

Jaime: Michael, your turn. Who are you and, while you're at it, just how did you get started in the newspaper game?

Michael: "You're going to pay me how much!?"

Working my first newspaper job, I earned eight pounds, three shillings a week, with the promise of a raise on my birthday. Happy to take it. That kind of money allowed me to buy a car older than I was. Seemed a big paycheque in 1969. I was just seventeen. It was against the law for me, but a warm pint of Mitchell's Best Bitter beer was just two shillings.

I'd left school at sixteen and decided the farm was actual hard work, so I'd signed on as an apprentice reporter at the *Morecambe Visitor*, our brilliantly named local weekly newspaper in the seaside town of Morecambe in northwest England.

From then 'til now: newspapers, newspapers, newspapers. More fun than a man should have, with better people than anyone could hope to call colleagues, bosses, leaders, employees, friends.

They taught me a lot.

Starting with Mr. Mosey.

Mr. Mosey, the editor at the *Visitor*, taught me to write short. "Leave out the bits people skip over, Michael." He also made me clean and polish his big glass ashtray full of smelly, filthy butts. One day, after two drags of a full-strength Senior Service cigarette, he doubles over coughing and says, "Michael," *cough-retch-cough*, "you've misspelled *grammar*. It's *grammar*, not *grammer* with an *e*. Do you know why you misspelled *grammar*? Because you're not as clever as you think you are. Get that tar scrubbed off my ashtray. And don't look at me like that. It's an imposition. It'll make you check your spelling."

Now that's what I call capital-letters LEADERSHIP.

I was a know-it-all teenager at the *Visitor* in the rebellious heady days of the sixties when post-Sinatra pop music was addictive. A girlfriend dumped me because of my obsession with The Monkees. I thought she was joking. And then I saw her face. Had a couple of years down on Fleet Street in London in the seventies where there were just a few women in newsrooms in a time when *harass* was two words. So weird to look back in time through the wrong end of a telescope.

Jaime: I know a guy if you need to talk more about Mr. Mosey. But, kidding aside, what happened when you crossed the pond? How did you get started in the "new world"?

Michael: I came to Toronto for a vacation, popped into the *Toronto Star* newsroom to see a pal, sat down, and did a desk shift on the copydesk. I never went back to the UK.

Early on I found out what it was like to be a reporter for the *Star*—there was a fire in the Saint John, NB, town jail. "A dozen dead!" the news editor shouted.

The *Star* had money and passion to get the news. We rented a Learjet to get our team to that tragedy. The guards made frantic phone calls trying to find the jailhouse key while teens caught joyriding were in with the drunks sleeping it off in the cells.

So many young men died. My first *Star* byline.

Fast-forward again, working at the *Montreal Gazette* as City Editor. We covered the first referendum on Québécois sovereignty, which Canada won handily. The second referendum was a squeaker, though!

Then a long flight across the Prairies to the *Journal*, in Edmonton. Two winters hitting minus forty, plugging in the car's block heater and hearing, "Oh, it's a dry cold . . ."

Then it was over the Rockies to lead the feisty underdogs at the *Province*, where we all got up an hour earlier and went to bed an hour later than those bums over at the *Vancouver Sun*.

Next stop: editor at the *Chicago Sun-Times*, which meant eight years of big cars, big buildings, big sports, big crime, big politics, big corruption, big news, and big people. Oprah was the biggest thing in town until Obama came along.

Then to be editor of the *New York Daily News* and the fizz and pop of tabloid craziness with the *New York Post* where I despised Donald Trump before you did. I have stories.

Returning to the *Toronto Star* in 2008, I completed the circle.

For me personally, nothing topped the story I wrote about fifteen-year-old Roya Shams in 2012—the thrill of flying to Kandahar to help smuggle her out under the eyes of the Taliban to her new life in Canada. She's doing great, by the way, completing her master's at Ottawa U. Google her! Roya is a reminder that even if journalism can't save everyone, if it can save one person, it's worth everything.

Me now? Thanks for asking. I left the *Toronto Star* three years ago and now work around the world—Mali, Bangladesh, Congo—helping and admiring the young journalists in developing countries who don't work for Mr. Mosey at the *Visitor* and have no ashtrays to scrub but who face challenges beyond anything I could imagine.

Jaime: You're a reporter guy, so let me follow up with a few direct questions. Have you ever liked columnists? And how about a critique of mine?

Michael: This is what I believed when I was a reporter: only after the reporters win the battle will the columnists, who've been hiding behind boulders and in bushes all this time, come down from the hillside to pick the pockets of the dead.

Tug off dead men's boots. Pull rings off fingers. Steal watches.

I was sure that was the way journalism worked until I wasn't. Until I became an editor and developed an appreciation that those columnists stooping and scurrying and collecting among the bodies also tell us why the battle was fought, who really won, and where the next fight will be. We need that.

I've never written a political column.

If I was to give it a go, I would inhale André Pratte's advice in the foreword to this book, a masterclass from a master columnist.

It was Mel Brooks who said, "If you're quiet, you're not living. You've got to be classy and smart and noisy and colourful and lively." That's André Pratte. Classy columns, often classical. He's his own Mozart to my Herman's Hermits.

And then there's you, Jaime. Classy smart noisy colourful lively. A triple-decker sandwich of intellect, understanding, and knowledge of current events and controversies, much of it gleaned from work at your company Navigator, the country's leading think-and-go-get-it-done tank.

You're able to write amazingly different columns on the same subject. Take Canadian aviation policy. Should we allow jets to land and take off at the Toronto Island airport, Billy Bishop? (My opinion: no). Or this: What is the biggest development of our time in air travel? (My opinion: those little wheels on suitcases.)

Those little wheels remind me about the arc of progress being uneven— we put men on the moon in 1969, but it was decades later until we figured out how our luggage could be more easily lugged. And that is a thing columnists should remember when they assess things in the moment, isn't it?

You've got to admire a writer with the confidence and candour to say *I got it wrong.* If more of us could so graciously admit that to ourselves and maybe say it out loud, well, that could be even better than wheels on suitcases.

That's what puts your book on the top shelf of contemporary Canadian political literature.

I'd happily spend two weeks with you in a windowless room tossing cards into an empty hat. I get that when you're not writing a column, when you're in your Navigator public-policy life, you live in intelligent greyness, which in your world is a synonym for decisive nuance. You're happy to admit you once were found and now are lost.

To be honest, that's a useless if honest stance for columnists. A friend who dabbled in opinion writing once told me the key was to have an opinion. Take a position, state it clearly, explain and defend it, pre-emptively rebut any easily anticipated responses, and then hit "send." It's just an opinion piece, not a Supreme Court judgment or even a final exam in an undergrad class. But you know column writing, and you do this gig well: find a subject, reflect briefly, then pull the trigger. Crucial in our business to kiss the deadline smack on the lips.

In your columns, you deliver delightful surprises and the occasional jolt of information that might make your life better on matters large and small. There's another sign of a top columnist—they tell you more than just their opinion. The best columns often draw blood. They add context, original reporting even. Martin Regg Cohn does this at the *Star.* Andrew Coyne at the *Globe.* Tasha Kheiriddin at the *National Post.*

Then there are the columnists who basically write, "Did you see this story yesterday? Here's what I think about it," and then don't add much. Or worse: "Did you see this three days ago?"

Columnists in Canada are divided into two groups: those who run with the bulls and those who live in a petting zoo. Matadors and doormats. Thankfully there are many who help readers *understand* the news. They're not trying to tell you what to think, they're just trying to get you to think.

Hey, they all want to persuade their readers, of course. But even if a column simply helps us firm up our thoughts in disagreement, it has done something valuable. To the readers out there: You have friends you discuss and argue with who sometimes change your view, right? While other times you become even firmer in your view? Well, if you don't, maybe get different friends.

Or, at least, read more Jaime Watt.

Jaime: Can a columnist's opinion or point of view get in the way of good writing?

Michael: Good writing like good music comes in many styles. I like a thin style that uses humour to deliver a point. But it don't mean a thing, if it ain't got that swing. I used to tell students they had to master clarity and understand rhythm. You can't play jazz until you can play basic chords.

I like the fundamental rule of three . . . it's how I best remember. Let's take the three things that, as an older man (older than you, Jaime!), I've yet to experience:

- Seeing a baby being born.
- Being present for a big archaeological find.
- Seeing a woman jump out of a cake.

I'll ask you, Jaime, when I see you next, what three things I said I've yet to experience. I bet you'll remember my trifecta.

The columnist's work delivering information starts where the politician's soundbite ends. Here's where style steps in. You can press the reader's nose deep into a swamp of stinky facts, or you can act the waiter and lift the silver cloche off the plate with a grin and a "Ta-dah! Here's something you'll enjoy."

Style takes years to develop, but when you have it, you can take it to the bank. Distinction is important. Try this: have someone clip ten columns from ten writers covering basically the same subject, take the bylines off, and see if you can tell who wrote what. The ones you recognize immediately, those writers have that swing.

Jaime: Sometimes when I write I think I am either talking to myself or to the folks with too much time on their hands who feel compelled to correspond with me. Have you ever seen column writing matter? Make a difference? Do columnists have power?

Michael: You want power? I'll tell you about power. I'll tell you about a newspaper column from 1973 still talked about today, written by *Chicago Daily News*'s Mike Royko.

Royko plowed solo through the soil of politics. Never stood in front of a podium taking notes in his life. In a column published December 10, 1973, he wrote about Leroy Bailey, who had his face blown off in Vietnam, who had to feed himself with a syringe, and whom the US Department of Veteran Affairs refused to pay for surgery, saying it was "cosmetic." Well, Nixon reacted to that column the next day.

Royko's writing is thin, muscled, beautiful, powerful, rhythmic, like verses from Ecclesiastes.

And remember we're reading him still today, now, in 2023, in the following excerpt from that fifty-year-old column.

> Until he was hit by a rocket, [Bailey] had teeth. Now he has none. He had eyes. Now he has none. He had a nose. Now he has none. People could look at him. Now most of them turn away.
>
> … If we can afford $5 million to make [Richard Nixon's] San Clemente property prettier, we can do whatever is humanly possible for this man's face.[77]

The headline in Royko's newspaper the very next day blared, "Nixon Reads Royko's Column; Orders VA to Aid Faceless Vet."

That still makes me stand up and applaud. And remember, back then Nixon was contemptuous of the media due to the Watergate scandal coverage, but this newspaper column made the president do an immediate one-eighty on what had been a firm government policy.

That sort of thing doesn't happen as much today. Best you can hope for is a government slightly *adjusting* a policy after an accumulation of newspaper opinions runs against them. Political column writing is not, for the most part, about getting action. It's about spreading knowledge and wisdom so that the readers—the voters—can take action.

Call me old-fashioned: I prefer the Royko way.

Jaime: I often write about leadership. In considering leadership and what makes a good leader, I have grown more uncertain. You are a leader, and you've worked with them your whole life. Have you got it figured out?

Michael: During my teenaged years, when I arrived in my first newsroom, there was a boss who had spent his own teenaged years trying to kill Germans.

Let's call him Angry Andy. But not to his face.

His every move and every sentence seemed shaped by WWII. Back in those days there was no such thing as PTSD. The only acronym he knew was FU.

What would set him off? Maybe my pink flared pants and pointy shoes. Or my Elvis sideburns and ruffled shirt front. Or my sprinkling of semicolons in my copy. He hated semicolons. Now, fifty years later, I can't stand them either.

Angry Andy ranted and raved. "Michael, you make the metal plate in my head get hot."

I didn't think he was joking.

And then he'd take the brush out of the news-desk glue pot and dab my nose.

The other reporters laughed.

I feared and admired Angry Andy in equal parts. What a role model for a cub reporter. Is it any wonder that when I became a newsroom boss myself, my definition of leadership was: *A lot of people doing exactly what I tell them to do.*

Of course, that never was the best way, and is less so today.

An effective leader is willing to say, "I honestly don't know." Another good option: "I don't know, but I will try to find out."

Leaders must listen. And then listen more. Have empathy. Try harder to have empathy. Question themselves and their assumptions. Let others have their way on things that aren't core. And certainly, no bullying. Learn how to say, "I was wrong" and even, "I'm sorry I dabbed glue on your nose."

Jaime: Try as I might, I haven't been able to stop writing about Donald Trump. Unfortunately for all of us, there are many paler facsimiles around—especially in business. Have you got one?

Michael: I don't know where you grew up or what you were doing when you were nine years old, but I grew up in an English village, and at nine, I was in a field watching a local farmer castrate sheep.

"What are you doing, Mr. Atkinson?" I asked.

"Well, lad," he said, "these here sheep are too young and small to have lambs born from them so I'm cutting out the lamb eggs. We'll pop them in the incubator where we put the turkey eggs. They'll hatch in a few weeks. Here, you can hold one."

Mr. Atkinson placed the steaming, gooey testicle in my palm.

"Can you feel the heart beating?" he asked.

"No, sir," I replied.

"Press it close to your ear . . . that's it! Press it closer. Now can you hear the heartbeat?"

He smirked and laughed. Later during the tea break, Mr. Atkinson's farmhands told me why they thought this was the funniest thing they'd ever seen.

Cruel? Tick.

Abuse of power? Tick.

Bullying? Tick.

Sound familiar? Sounds very Trumpy to me.

Four decades later, I met the man—Donald J. Trump—himself. I won't go into details here, but it involved real estate and some serious hoodwinking on his part that unjustly moved a large sum from my wallet to his. Of course, Trump didn't just deceive me. Trump has ripped off thousands of people around the world. Abusing smaller people is what he does.

Mr. Atkinson never got near the nuclear launch button, or tried to wreck NATO, or let Putin loose, or—as far as I know—did any of the other appalling things (pick your own example) that Trump did while president. I preferred the encounter with Mr. Atkinson.

Jaime: Since leaving the *Toronto Star*, you have made an amazing commitment to civil liberties and human rights, especially expressed in the context of journalists trying to do their work all over the world. What are the most worrisome threats you see? What kind of questions should we be asking?

Michael: A few years ago, I met a guy in the middle of the Congo, his name was Richard Kawaya. This is what he told me:

"When the militiamen came to my village, they cut off the heads of six men and made me pick up the heads and put them in their sacks.

"And then they gave me a choice:

"I could be decapitated . . . or I could be burned.

"I chose to be burned."

They held him down and Mr. Kawaya had red-hot charcoal dumped on his legs.

He rolled up his pants to show me his wounds. Take a photograph, he said. I did. I don't think you want to see it.

Someone else who saw the killings and maimings and rapes said:

"How can I tell you? The violence was so terrible, we didn't hear the birds sing for days."

Millions of people driven from their homes. Tens of thousands maimed. Thousands dead.

So, Jaime, you ask about the biggest coming threats to human rights and civil liberties. On what basis? Numbers of people affected? Their causes?

Over here, great lakes of ink gush into columns decrying the glass ceiling or shouting for more affirmative action. But there's rarely a speck of ink given to Mr. Kawaya and the countless others who suffer in the fighting triggered by our lust for African mineral resources.

Much of the world's supply of the critical minerals required for our phones and our new electric cars is in the ground in Congo. This causes internal wars, suffering, and displacement that Western media and governments, including our own, don't talk about. Why don't we care? Because

Congo does not have a geographic or ethnic proximity to Canada. In other words, the Congolese are not like us and their country is a long way away.

The situation in Congo is a bigger human rights crisis than what has been happening in Syria or Afghanistan or Ukraine in terms of humans killed and tortured or turned overnight into refugees in their own countries.

Because of "ethnic proximity," we've prioritized the human rights of the Ukrainian people above all other crises, which, says Rachel Pulfer, executive director of the Toronto-based Journalists for Human Rights, pushes the BRICS countries (Brazil, Russia, India, China, South Africa) and non-aligned states toward a more totalitarian way of life. BRICS also see the heavy focus on Ukraine as hypocritical in that other human rights abuses don't get as much attention.

What are the biggest threats to human rights and civil liberties? Start in the Congo and ripple it out. This could be a good column for you, Jaime. Let me know if you want me to be your researcher.

Jaime: You have got yourself a deal. Thanks, you are always amazing. You never disappoint.

Endnotes

Part 1: Civil Liberties and Human Rights

1. Health Infobase, "Opioid- and Stimulant-Related Harms in Canada," *Government of Canada*, March 2023, https://health-infobase.canada.ca/substance-related-harms/opioids-stimulants/.

2. Kendra Mangione and Bhinder Sajan, "Hate Crimes Up 97 Percent Overall in Vancouver Last Year, Anti-Asian Hate Crimes Up 717 Percent," *CTV News*, February 18, 2021, https://bc.ctvnews.ca/hate-crimes-up-97-overall-in-vancouver-last-year-anti-asian-hate-crimes-up-717-1.5314307.

3. Kathleen Harris, "Canada Loses Its Bid for Seat on UN Security Council," *CBC News*, June 18, 2020, https://www.cbc.ca/news/politics/united-nations-security-council-canada-1.5615488#.

4. Diane R. Davidson and Miriam Lapp, Electoral Insight: Persons with Disabilities and Elections," *Elections Canada*, April 2004, https://www.elections.ca/content.aspx?section=res&dir=eim/issue10&document=p4&lang=e.

5. Ryan Mac and Craig Silverman, "Plunging Morale and Self-Congratulations: Inside Facebook the Day Before the Presidential Election," *Buzzfeed News*, November 2, 2020, https://www.buzzfeednews.com/article/ryanmac/inside-facebook-24-hours-before-election-day.

6. Mickey Djuric, "As Content Creators Await the Passing of Bill C-11, Some Say It's Still Too Ambiguous," *CTV News*, April 10, 2023, https://www.ctvnews.ca/politics/as-content-creators-await-the-passing-of-bill-c-11-some-say-it-s-still-too-ambiguous-1.6349475.

7. Daniel Otis, "What Is Bill C-18, And How Do I Know If Google Is Blocking My News Content?" *CTV News*, February 24, 2023, https://www.ctvnews.ca/politics/what-is-bill-c-18-and-how-do-i-know-if-google-is-blocking-my-news-content-1.6286816.

8. Marie Woolf, "Lifetime Ban for Sex Workers Donating Blood Should Be Scrapped: Canadian Blood Services," *Global News*, May 27, 2022, https://globalnews.ca/news/8874328/canadian-blood-services-sex-worker-blood-ban/.

9. "Fulton v. City of Philadelphia," American Civil Liberties Union (website), last modified November 21, 2021, https://www.aclu.org/cases/fulton-v-city-philadelphia.

10. Marjan Sadat, "'I Have Decided to Sacrifice: This Afghan Journalist Is Taking Drastic Measures to Support His Family. And He Isn't Alone," *Toronto Star*, February 19, 2023, https://www.thestar.com/news/world/2023/02/19/i-have-decided-to-sacrifice-this-afghan-journalist-is-taking-drastic-measures-to-support-his-family-and-he-isnt-alone.html.

11. Spencer J. Cox, "Why I'm Vetoing HB11," Utah Governor Spencer J. Cox's website, last modified March 24, 2022, https://governor.utah.gov/2022/03/24/gov-cox-why-im-vetoing-hb11/.

12. Alex Seitz-Wald and Jo Yurcaba, "Trump Vows to 'Stop' Gender-Affirming Care for Minors If Re-elected President," *NBC News*, January 31, 2023, https://www.nbcnews.com/politics/2024-election/trump-vows-stop-gender-affirming-care-minors-re-elected-president-rcna68461.

Part 2: Portraits of Leadership

13. Mark Twain (Samuel Clemens), *Following the Equator: A Journey Around the World* (Hartford: The American Publishing Company, 1897; Project Gutenberg, May 25, 2018), https://www.gutenberg.org/files/2895/2895-h/2895-h.htm.

14. Paul Dewar, "Paul Dewar Says Goodbye," *CBC News*, February 6, 2019, https://www.cbc.ca/news/canada/ottawa/paul-dewar-says-goodbye-facebook-post-1.5008897.

15. Édouard Louis, *Speaking of Democracy*, presented by the Honourable Elizabeth Dowdeswell in co-operation with the Samara Centre for Democracy, April 23, 2019, http://arts.lgontario.ca/democracy-democratie/wp-content/uploads/sites/13/2019/04/LGO_Speaking_of_Democracy_EN.pdf.

16. Jean Augustine, Elizabeth Dowdeswell, and Elizabeth May, interview by Nam Kiwanuka, "Leadership Insights from Female Trailblazers," *TVO Today*, August 17, 2021, https://www.tvo.org/transcript/2668446.

17. Chelsea Nash, "MPs Agree to Parliamentary Probe of McKinsey Contracts, Calling On Dominic Barton and Seven Ministers to Appear," *The Hill Times*, January 18, 2023, https://www.hilltimes.com/story/2023/01/18/mps-agree-to-parliamentary-probe-of-mckinsey-contracts-calling-on-dominic-barton-and-seven-ministers-to-appear/361536/.

18. Theodore Roosevelt, "Speech at the Sorbonne," April 23, 1910, Paris, France, quoted in "It Is Not the Critic Who Counts," Theodore Roosevelt Conservation Partnership (website), January 18, 2011, https://www.trcp.org/2011/01/18/it-is-not-the-critic-who-counts/.

19. Rosie DiManno, "Prince Andrew's Attempt to Dismiss Sex Assault Case Hits Road Blocks," *Toronto Star*, January 4, 2022, https://www.thestar.com/opinion/star-columnists/2022/01/04/prince-andrews-attempt-to-dismiss-sex-assault-case-hits-roadblocks.html.

20. Emily Maitlis, "Prince Andrew: Emily Maitlis Says Duke's Interview Answers Are Critical to Sex Assault Case," *BBC News*, January 4, 2022, https://www.bbc.com/news/uk-59874170.

21. Prince Andrew, Duke of York, interview by Emily Maitlis, "Prince Andrew and the Epstein Scandal: The Newsnight Interview," *BBC News*, November 17, 2019, YouTube video, 49:26, https://www.youtube.com/watch?v=QtBS8COhhhM.

22. Kenzie Bryant, "The Genuine Shock of that Prince Harry Frostbite Story," *Vanity Fair*, January 6, 2023, https://www.vanityfair.com/style/2023/01/prince-harry-frostbite-story.

23. Jill Lawless, "Has Rule-Breaker Boris Johnson Met His Match in 'Partygate'?" *Toronto Star*, January 21, 2022, https://www.thestar.com/news/world/europe/2022/01/21/has-rule-breaker-boris-johnson-met-his-match-in-partygate.html.

24. Danica Kirka and Jill Lawless, "The Queen Says Goodbye to Philip, Continues Her Reign Alone," *Toronto Star*, April 17, 2021, https://www.thestar.com/news/world/2021/04/17/funeral-to-praise-philips-courage-and-support-for-queen.html.

25. Robert Rowlands, "Boris Johnson Close to Tears As He Apologizes to Queen As He Is Repeatedly Asked If He Will Resign," *Coventry Telegraph*, January 18, 2022, https://www.coventrytelegraph.net/news/boris-johnson-close-tears-apologises-22793932.

26. Sylvia Hui, "UK Lifts COVID Restrictions, Says Omicron Wave 'Has Peaked,'" *Toronto Star*, January 19, 2022, https://www.thestar.com/news/world/2022/01/19/uk-lifts-covid-restrictions-says-omicron-wave-has-peaked.html.

27. Jim Waterson, "Lettuce Rejoice: Inside Story of *Daily Star Iceberg's Triumph Over Liz Truss*," *The Guardian*, October 21, 2022, https://www.theguardian.com/media/2022/oct/21/inside-story-daily-star-lettuce-triumph-liz-truss.

28. "Easter Recess: Government Update," UK Parliament, Hansard, House of Commons debate, vol. 712, April 19, 2022, https://hansard.parliament.uk/commons/2022-04-19/debates/2C3E878D-6ECB-4FF2-9E3A-7B134989EAA6/EasterRecessGovernmentUpdate.

29. Farnaz Fassihi, "The UN Security Council Met to Prevent Military Action by Putin. Russia Invaded Ukraine As They Spoke," *The New York Times*, February 24, 2022, https://www.nytimes.com/2022/02/24/world/europe/un-security-council-russia-ukraine.html.

30. John Galsworthy, *Strife: Idealism Increases in Direct Proportion to One's Distance from the Problem* (Stage Door: 2017).

Part 3: In Power

31. Maggie Severns, "Trump Pins NAFTA, 'Worst Trade Deal Ever,' On Clinton," *Politico*, September 26, 2016, https://www.politico.com/story/2016/09/trump-clinton-come-out-swinging-over-nafta-228712.

32. "Doug Ford Has Won Ontario's Election. What Happens Now? A Guide," *The Globe and Mail*, June 8, 2018, https://www.theglobeandmail.com/canada/article-doug-ford-wins-ontario-election-explainer/.

33. Stephen Azzi, "Election of 1988," September 2, 2015, *The Canadian Encyclopedia*, https://www.thecanadianencyclopedia.ca/en/article/election-1988-feature.

34. Emma Celeste Thornley, "Democracy Notwithstanding: Canada's History of the Notwithstanding Clause and Its Role in Human Rights," *Candlelight*, Amnesty International at the University of Toronto, January 31, 2023, https://amnesty.sa.utoronto.ca/2023/01/31/democracy-notwithstanding-canadas-history-of-the-notwithstanding-clause-and-its-role-in-human-rights/#.

35. Matt Lundy, November 26, 2022, "Canada Wants to Welcome Five Hundred Thousand Immigrants a Year by 2022. Can Our Country Keep Up?" *The Globe and Mail*, November 26, 2022, https://www.theglobeandmail.com/business/article-canada-immigration-population-boom/.

36. "The Twentieth Century Belongs to Canada," *Parli: The Dictionary of Canadian Politics*, accessed May 9, 2023, https://parli.ca/twentieth-century-belongs-canada/.

Part 4: In Opposition

37. Éric Grenier, "Popular Vote Numbers Reveal Wider Margin of Victory for Andrew Scheer," *CBC News*, May 29, 2017, https://www.cbc.ca/news/politics/grenier-conservative-popvote-1.4136812.

38. "Conservatives Gain Twenty-Six Seats, Win Popular Vote," *Global News*, October 22, 2019, https://globalnews.ca/video/6069434/conservatives-gain-26-seats-win-popular-vote/.

39. Henry Nevinson, *Essays in Rebellion* (London: James Nisbet & Co. Ltd., 1913; Project Gutenberg, February 14, 2004), https://www.gutenberg.org/files/11079/11079-h/11079-h.htm.

40. Maggie Astor, "Elizabeth Warren, Criticizing Bloomberg, Sent a Message: She Won't Be Ignored," *The New York Times*, February 19, 2020, https://www.nytimes.com/2020/02/19/us/politics/elizabeth-warren-debate.html.

41. This quote is apocryphal. "Alexandre Auguste Ledru-Rollin (1807–74)," *Bartleby*, accessed May 9, 2023, https://www.bartleby.com/lit-hub/respectfully-quoted/alexandre-auguste-ledru-rollin-180774/.

42. Aaron D'Andrea, "NDP's Singh Calls for Inquiry on Alleged China Election Interference," *Global News*, February 27, 2023, https://globalnews.ca/news/9513589/ndp-singh-public-inquiry-china-interference-call/.

43. Peter Zimonjic, "Conservatives, NDP Criticize Budget's Impact on People, Businesses as Trudeau Defends Measures," *CBC News*, March 29, 2023, https://www.cbc.ca/news/politics/opposition-reaction-to-federal-budget-1.6795130.

44. Susan Delacourt, "Steam Whistle, Pierre Poilievre, and Canada's Toxic Partisanship," *Toronto Star*, April 20, 2022, https://www.thestar.com/politics/political-opinion/2022/04/20/steam-whistle-pierre-poilievre-and-canadas-toxic-partisanship.html.

45. Ian Bailey, "Pierre Poilievre Draws Crowds, But That Isn't Crucial for Winning," *The Globe and Mail*, April 18, 2022, https://www.theglobeandmail.com/politics/article-pierre-poilievre-draws-crowds-but-that-isnt-crucial-for-winning/.

46. The Associated Press, "2022 Midterms Live Updates: Latest Elections News from AP," *Toronto Star*, November 9, 2022, https://www.thestar.com/news/world/us/2022/11/09/2022-midterms-live-updates-latest-election-news-from-ap.html.

47. Rick Salutin, "On US Midterm Results, It's Refreshing When You Get So Many Expectations Wrong," *Toronto Star*, November 11, 2022, https://www.thestar.com/opinion/contributors/2022/11/11/on-us-midterm-results-its-refreshing-when-you-get-so-many-expectations-wrong.html.

48. Laura Dawson, Post-Midterms, Canada Should Expect Little From a Divided US," *Toronto Star*, November 11, 2022, https://www.thestar.com/opinion/contributors/2022/11/11/post-midterms-canada-should-expect-little-from-a-divided-us.html.

49. Thomas Walkom, "Did the US Midterms Represent the Beginning of the End for Donald Trump?" *Toronto Star*, November 11, 2022, https://www.thestar.com/opinion/contributors/2022/11/11/did-the-us-midterms-represent-the-beginning-of-the-end-for-donald-trump-dont-bet-on-it.html.

50. The Associated Press, "'A Disaster': Speaker Fight Exposes GOP Leadership Vacuum," *US News*, January 5, 2023, https://www.usnews.com/news/politics/articles/2023-01-05/a-disaster-speaker-fight-exposes-gop-leadership-vacuum.

51. Amy Walter, "Why Are Republicans Going After 'Wokeness' Instead of Going After Biden," *The Cook Political Report*, February 23, 2023, https://www.cookpolitical.com/analysis/national/national-politics/why-are-republicans-going-after-wokeness-instead-going-after.

Part 5: The Trump Years

52. An updated tip-of-the-hat to Terry Mosher's famous "Okay, everyone, take a Valium" cartoon after Parti Québécois leader René Lévesque was elected the country's first separatist premier.

53. Ingrid Jacques, "What Does 'Woke' Mean? For Conservatives, It's So Much More Than Political Correctness," *USA Today*, March 10, 2023, https://www.usatoday.com/story/opinion/columnist/2023/03/10/what-does-woke-mean-republicans/11427923002/.

54. Lisa Lerer and Reid J. Epstein, "Abandon Trump? Deep in the GOP Ranks, The MAGA Mindset Prevails," *The New York Times*, January 21, 2021, https://www.nytimes.com/2021/01/14/us/politics/trump-republicans.html.

55. Richard Hall, Texas Republicans Want to Secede from the United States. Could They Do It?" *The Independent*, June 20, 2022, https://www.independent.co.uk/news/world/americas/us-politics/texas-secession-republicans-donald-trump-b2105461.html.

56. Plan International, "G7 Girls' Education Declaration Will Be Another Empty Promise Unless UK Aid Cuts Are Reversed," *ReliefWeb*, May 5, 2021, https://reliefweb.int/report/world/g7-girls-education-declaration-will-be-another-empty-promise-unless-uk-aid-cuts-are.

57. "Sweden's Right-Wing Announces New Government with Far-Right Backing," *Le Monde*, October 14, 2022, https://www.lemonde.fr/en/europe/article/2022/10/14/sweden-s-right-wing-announces-new-government-with-far-right-backing_6000299_143.html.

58. Jon Henley, "Finland's Conservatives to Open Coalition Talks with Far-Right Party," *The Guardian*, April 27, 2023, https://www.theguardian.com/world/2023/apr/27/finland-petteri-orpo-coalition-far-right-finns-party.

Part 6: The COVID-19 Crisis

59. The Associated Press, "WHO Downgrades COVID Pandemic, Says It's No Longer a Global Emergency," *CBC News*, May 5, 2023, https://www.cbc.ca/news/health/who-pandemic-not-emergency-1.6833321.

60. "Pandemic Threatens Decades of Women's Labour Force Gains," *RBC Economics*, July 16, 2020, https://thoughtleadership.rbc.com/pandemic-threatens-decades-of-womens-labour-force-gains/.

61. "Table 9: Homicides, By Closest Accused to Victim Relationship and Gender, Canada, 2020," *Statistics Canada*, November 25, 2021, https://www150.statcan.gc.ca/n1/pub/85-002-x/2021001/article/00017/tbl/tbl09-eng.htm.

62. Anna Mehler Paperny, "Canada's Use of Emergency Powers During 'Freedom Convoy' Met Threshold, Commissioner Says," *Reuters*, February 17, 2023, https://www.reuters.com/world/americas/canadas-use-emergency-powers-during-freedom-convoy-met-threshold-commissioner-2023-02-17/.

63. Greg Allen, "Presidential Runner-Up Gaffes," *Journal Review*, August 7, 2012, https://www.journalreview.com/stories/refusing-to-play-by-the-rules,39155.

64. Bob Hepburn, "Suddenly, Crime Emerges as Top Issue in Toronto Mayoral Race," *Toronto Star*, March 30, 2023, https://www.thestar.com/opinion/star-columnists/2023/03/30/suddenly-crime-emerges-as-top-issue-in-toronto-mayoral-race.html.

65. Maria Weisgarber, "Vancouver Mayor Promises Two Hundred Thousand–Plus Homes Over Ten Years If Re-elected, Opponents Slam Proposal," *CTV News*, https://bc.ctvnews.ca/vancouver-mayor-promises-200-000-homes-over-10-years-if-re-elected-opponents-slam-proposal-1.6067598.

66. Catlin de Villa, "Private Landlords Are Not to Blame for Housing Crisis," *Toronto Star*, March 6, 2023, https://www.thestar.com/opinion/contributors/2023/03/06/private-landlords-are-not-to-blame-for-housing-crisis.html.

67. "Storm Without End: The Economic and Fiscal Impact of COVID in Canada," *Fraser Institute*, October 12, 2022, https://www.fraserinstitute.org/studies/storm-without-end-the-economic-and-fiscal-impact-of-covid-in-canada.

68. "Government Spending By Function," November 25, 2022, *Statistics Canada*, https://www150.statcan.gc.ca/n1/daily-quotidien/221125/dq221125a-eng.htm.

69. "2022 Reports 9 and 10 of the Auditor General of Canada to the Parliament of Canada," *Office of the Auditor General of Canada*, November 1, 2022, https://www.oag-bvg.gc.ca/internet/English/parl_oag_202212_10_e_44176.html.

70. M. K. Gandhi, *An Autobiography or The Story of My Experiments with Truth*, trans. Mahadev Desai (New Haven: Yale University Press, 2018), https://www.sas.upenn.edu/~cavitch/pdf-library/Gandhi_Autobiography.pdf.

71. Benjamin Wittes, interview by Robert Siegel, "Ben Franklin's Famous 'Liberty, Safety' Quote Lost Its Context in Twenty-First Century," *NPR*, March 2, 2015, https://www.npr.org/2015/03/02/390245038/ben-franklins-famous-liberty-safety-quote-lost-its-context-in-21st-century.

72. Fatema Tokhy, "The World Must Regulate China's Wet Markets," *Toronto Star*, May 20, 2020, https://www.thestar.com/opinion/contributors/2020/05/20/the-world-must-regulate-chinas-wet-markets.html.

73. Zeke Miller and Aamer Madhani, "Biden Orders More Intel Investigation of COVID-19 Origin," *Toronto Star*, May 26, 2021, https://www.thestar.com/news/world/us/2021/05/26/biden-asks-us-intel-community-to-investigate-covid-19-origin.html.

74. Daniel Funke, "Tucker Carlson Guest Airs Debunked Conspiracy Theory That COVID-19 Was Created in a Lab," *Politifact*, September 16, 2020, https://www.politifact.com/li-meng-yan-fact-check/.

75. Edward Helmore, "COVID-19 Likely Came from Lab Leak, Says News Report Citing US Energy Department," *The Guardian*, February 26, 2023, https://www.theguardian.com/world/2023/feb/26/covid-virus-likely-laboratory-leak-us-energy-department.

Epilogue: One Last Thing

76. Avis Favaro, "New Service Aims to Match Living Kidney Donors with Canadians in Need of Life-Saving Transplants, *CTV News*, July 21, 2022, https://www.ctvnews.ca/health/new-service-aims-to-match-living-kidney-donors-with-canadians-in-need-of-life-saving-transplants-1.5996576.

77. Mike Royko, "A Faceless Man's Plea," *The Chicago Daily News*, December 10, 1973, https://docs.google.com/viewer?a=v&pid=sites&srcid=cHZsZW-Fybm Vycy5uZXR8Z2NoYXZlemhvbm9yc3xneDo3MDJlMDUxN-zA3MDY2YzE5.